BLACK
UTAH

BLACK UTAH

Stories from a Thriving Community

UTAH BLACK CHAMBER

Interior design by THE COSMIC LION

ISBN 978-1-7372000-7-9 (color print)
ISBN 978-1-7372000-9-3 (black & white print)
ISBN 978-1-7372000-8-6 (ebook)

With Special Thanks To:

INTERVIEWS:

Young OG Perspective

SPONSORS:

Workers Compensation Fund
Intermountain Healthcare
Zions Bank

Contents

FOUR

Small Business Leadership

FIVE

Emerging Leaders

SIX

Utah Native

SEVEN

Raising a Family in Utah

EIGHT

Arts, Dining, and Entertainment

NINE

Religious Leadership

BLACK UTAH

Introduction

The best snow on Earth with arguably the best mountain lands in the country. Five national parks full of amazing hiking trails, mountain and rock formations, and majestic landscapes. Business reviews and economists rank Utah the top in the country for business and opportunity. The home base of the LDS Church. This is usually how Utah is identified. What is not associated with Utah is diversity, particularly, a home to African Americans.

As a native Utahn, I never knew or understood an environment where African Americans were the majority of the population. I have visited many minority majority places to get a taste of what it would be like, but it was never enough to take me away from Utah. Everything mentioned at the beginning has created incredible opportunities for me and my family.

The mission of the Utah Black Chamber is to make these opportunities more visible and create more—to show Utah in a different light than what has been perceived. Utah has many Black citizens not just surviving but thriving, being pioneers for change, and creating a culture for all of us to call Utah home.

What most do not know is that Utah has been home to African

*The Utah Black Chamber and the Small Business Administration
signing of their Strategic Alliance Memorandum Agreement*

Americans even before the LDS pioneers arrived in Utah's territory in 1847. Twenty-five years prior to Brigham Young arriving, James Beckwourth joined the Rocky Mountain Fur Company in Cache Valley of Northern Utah. He became known as a prominent fur trapper and mountain man. He was known for his folklore adventures. He claims he was captured by the Crow tribe thinking he was the lost son of a Crow chief. While living with the Crow people, he rose to the position of Crow chief. Later in life, Beckwourth discovered the Beckwourth Pass, a low-elevation pass through the Sierra Nevada. It was originally a Native American pass through the mountains. He improved the trail to allow people to travel more quickly and safely.

Brigham Young came into Utah with three slaves that still have ancestors in Utah to this day. The names of Oscar Crosby, Hark Lay, and Green Flake are inscribed on a tablet on a Brigham Young monument in the middle of downtown Salt Lake City, in the intersection next to the Salt Lake Temple. These were the first three African

Americans to arrive in Utah territory. When Brigham Young became ill near the present Utah–Wyoming border, Green Flake—as well as Hark Lay and Oscar Crosby—joined a group of men under Orson Pratt's leadership to find the best route through the mountains to their destination in the valley. They formed what is known as the advance company. There were over a half-dozen Black families that arrived with Brigham Young, and Green Flake was recorded to have been the leading figure among the families and maintained a friendly relationship with Brigham Young until he died in 1847. Not much is known about Crosby and Lay. Both men traveled to Utah with a group of Mississippi Mormons that made a difficult journey from the South to Winter Quarters and then west with the first pioneer company in 1847. Like Green Flake, Crosby and Lay helped forge a road through Emigration Canyon and worked to establish the initial settlement in the Salt Lake Valley. By the end of 1847, it's recorded that there were perhaps a dozen African Americans living in Utah. From that small number, the Black community would grow and change during the next century and a half.*

The military was the next expansion of Utah's Black community. Between 1866 and 1900, the Black 9th Calvary troops of Fort Duchesne of eastern Utah were brought in to fight the restless Ute tribe. The Native Americans named these troops Buffalo Soldiers, for their dark curly hair and the way they fought resembled that of a buffalo.

In 1896, Fort Douglas in Salt Lake City brought six hundred Buffalo Soldiers through the 24th Infantry. Their families quadrupled the

---

* Sources: Ronald G. Coleman, "A History of Blacks in Utah, 1825–1910" (Ph.D. diss., University of Utah, 1980); Leonard J. Arrington, "Black Pioneer was Union Fort Settler," *The Pioneer* (SUP), September–October 1981.

People dancing at Evening in Harlem, the Utah Black Chamber's annual gala

city's Black population. American society was highly polarized by race in the 1890s, and Utah was no exception. Most African Americans still lived in the former slave states of the South, where they experienced severe restrictions on their social and legal rights, including frequent violence. Salt Lake City's small African American community did not experience much outright violence, but Utah's white population generally considered blacks second-class citizens. Minstrel shows, jokes, advertisements, and police behavior toward blacks demonstrated this attitude and reinforced negative racial stereotypes.*

After the Emancipation Proclamation, the railroad jobs were the best paying jobs for Black Americans, although they were paid

---

* Jeffrey D. Nichols, *History Blazer*, February 1995.

significantly less than the white railroad works. In 1869, the Ogden Union Station recruited emancipated slaves to work on the railroad. Black and Chinese railroad workers played an integral part in the development of the Transcontinental Railroad. The railroad workers worked on the ties and tracks and inside the railroad cars. They were cooks, porters, and waiters.

The growth of the Black railroad employees gave birth to a Black ecosystem in Ogden, Utah. A couple of the most prominent Black businesses were the hotel and the Porter and Waiters Club. The club was a host to many popular jazz musicians during that time, such as Duke Ellington, Count Basie, Nat King Cole, Louis Armstrong, Cab Calloway, and Ray Charles. Joe McQueen, a local jazz legend, performed with many of these artists. McQueen was a saxophonist from Dallas, Texas, who arrived in Utah in 1945. He toured with bands around the country, found a home in Utah, and played saxophone in clubs, solo, and with his own band up until he died at the age of 100 in 2019.

The porters and waiters would come to this club as other establishments didn't allow African Americans at the time. The Porters and Waiters Club would allow the railroad employees to not only enjoy the entertainment but stay overnight. It was the only outlet for jazz or Black entertainment in the state at the time. Black musicians were denied to play anywhere else and would come to the club to perform for their fans.

The military and railroad gave way to the growth of Black Utah. When the Utah Black Chamber was founded in 2009, the Black population was less than 1 percent. Due to the growth of Utah's economy, the Black community experienced another surge in growth to 2014, doubling the population again. As Utah continually grows, and attracts more professionals from out of state, many Black Americans have been contacting the Black Chamber about the Black experience in Utah. Questions would be asked like: Is it safe? How are the Mormons? Do Black people live there? Where do I go to church? Get a haircut? They are inquiring if there's a community for them.

This book will share the community that is here for the Black community. Hear from dozens of individuals with different backgrounds and experiences sharing why Utah has a community for them and how they are thriving. Hundreds could have shared valuable stories for this book. This is just a sample of a small but growing community.

James Jackson III
Founder Utah Black Chamber

BL4CK (4 Black) event at Salt Lake's Capitol

ONE

Corporate Leadership

In the early years of the Utah Black Chamber, the leadership asked the question "Who is the most successful Black business person in Utah?" The answer was complex. We knew there were successful Black entrepreneurs and businesspeople, but they weren't very visible in the community. The trailblazers for our community were traditionally educators, pastors, and community organizers. A business platform was not truly developed. Black businesses existed, and some were growing, but the overall Black business economy needed support.

An important element in the growth of a diverse community is allowing members of that community to see reflections of themselves in the roles they aspire to. Throughout history, and even now, we see many firsts. We are beginning to see diversity grow in everything around us. For Utah's Black business community to continue to grow, we need to spotlight successes from other business leaders.

While Black in leadership is still not where we desire it to be, our Black business leaders have become more visible, becoming pioneers for change. Seeing ourselves in more influential positions creates momentum.

Several years ago, the National Association of Black Accountants held their regional conference in Salt Lake City. They were hosted by one of the large financial firms that have a huge presence in downtown Salt Lake. Having the presence of over 100 Black financial executives in one room in a downtown Salt Lake building was an experience I didn't see forthcoming for several more years. Many of the attendees enjoyed Salt Lake and were in awe of the mountains and impressed with the hospitality of their hosts. A permanent presence like this would significantly elevate Utah's influence throughout the country. More diversity at the table creates more opportunities for diversity, which creates more opportunities for growth.

Utah has been consistently ranked at the top for its economy and as a place to start a small business. These are just a couple of reasons why Utah continues to attract people from all over the country and the world. Major corporations are relocating or expanding in Utah. At the same time, however, the state has lost significant opportunities because companies still are choosing other places with greater diversity. Diversity is a key indicator of a strong and growing community for many corporations. They want to be able to gain perspectives from all viewpoints, so they can be more innovative and more reflective of the market they serve. The most effective way to help elevate Utah's diversity and truly share how Utah is changing is to add more voices of color to the decision table.

I recall a few years ago attending a one day summit where many of Utah's leaders gathered to listen and be informed of the policies impacting the economy in the upcoming legislative session. Out of an attendance of nearly 800 people, there were only two Black people; myself and a reporter. I made a commitment to try to change that. The following year, the Utah Black Chamber purchased a table at this event and invited some of Utah's Black leaders and continued to do that every year. Over time, we began to see more diversity at this summit and many other similar events.

Utah is positioned and ready for more diversity at the table. We now see it as a priority in state government leadership, corporate recruitment, as well as identifying resources and organizations that can assist in strengthening and navigating this process. We also are beginning to see Black business leaders become more visible and engaging in the community recognizing the need for leadership and mentorship. We may not have the large Black corporations or Black-owned banks, but the foundation has been developed for more Black executives to come here and take advantage of the opportunities constantly growing here.

A five-time CEO and a success in a field where African Americans are underrepresented, Roy Banks is a trailblazer, maybe even in more ways than he realizes. He's firmly established here, a resident of Utah for about thirty years and a father of six living in Utah County since 1999. He's eager to reach out to the next generation, and now he's working with the Utah Black Chamber to help him expand his impact.

Roy is the definition of a visionary, someone who is able to see possibilities where others only see obstacles. His first big break came when he was willing to take a chance on a little known startup that had a vision for the future of the internet. It sold for more than a half-billion dollars less than a decade after he signed on. Fast forward a few more companies, and he is now the CEO at the helm of Weave, a SaaS-based communication and engagement technology company headquartered in Lehi, Utah, and he is positioning the company to grow to one thousand employees, with a deep commitment to diversity and inclusion.

We're happy to say that this visionary also sees promise in Utah.

JAMES: *Welcome, Roy. Tell us a little about your background.*

ROY: I'm a software engineer by trade and went to work back in the mid-nineties at a company called WordPerfect. I served in the Navy for five years before I moved to Utah: I was stationed in San Diego and New Orleans, where I was for most of my enlistment period.

I was a software engineer, and I loved it. I was also in a luxurious security force race to do VIP security for dignitaries in the

CEO Roy Banks at the NYSE announcement of Weave's initial public offering

southeast Gulf Coast of the United States, so I got to do security duty for the Air Force One and work with the Secret Service. But New Orleans was hot and humid, and San Diego, where I went to boot camp and did my schooling, was expensive.

Had I not been married, I probably would have stayed, but it's a tough life. My next deployment was a ship, so I decided to get out and proceed with my civilian career. What brought me to Utah was my wife. Her family moved here, and I was a software engineer. And at that time, I wasn't familiar with a lot of software companies, but my wife wanted to be close to her family. So I went to work at WordPerfect in Utah County.

I had gone to work and started my career in technology and then joined the military because I wanted the GI Bill to pay for college. You know, I grew up in a situation where we were just socioeconomically disadvantaged and didn't have a lot of opportunity. When I graduated from high school, I had tried to hold down a job and go to school, and I got married young, and I just needed to find my way. So the Navy was an outstanding option for me. They trained me in software engineering, and I went to Utah Valley University. I think I was probably one of the first African Americans to graduate from UVU with a bachelor's degree when they first opened their baccalaureate program.

JAMES: *How did your career take shape here in Utah?*

ROY: So let me tell you how it started. I was a software engineer at WordPerfect. I loved it, but I knew I wanted more. I knew I wanted to be in management. I knew I wanted to occupy a more important seat at the table. I wanted to be a decision-maker.

So what did I do? I just started managing my career and looking for different opportunities. In 1998, I had a chance to join a small startup, Authorize.net. Let me tell you about what this company was doing. At that time, the internet was not what we know it to be today. It was not this e-commerce medium. The internet was this ethereal network where you went if you wanted information, to either search for it or present it. This idea of selling goods and services and accepting payment for products and goods and services that you sell—that was not possible.

So this young man in Provo decided that he was going to basically make it possible to type a credit card form into a webform on a web page and accept payments and process it just like a point of sale device does in a retail location. When I first heard it, I was like, *That's the craziest thing ever.* Why would somebody want to do that? And so I rebuffed that, but I was still recruited to join this company. At the time, I was working for a company as a vice president of marketing. And I got contacted by Authorize.net again three or four months later. They said, "Hey, Roy, this thing's taken off." I saw, for the first time in my life, transformational and disruptive technology. I was like, *This is going to change your world.* So I joined the company. And let me tell you, after nine years, we sold the company for $662 million.

I had no idea that I would be part of a revolution. We ended up ushering in a whole new evolution in the industrial revolution that transformed and expanded the whole idea of commerce. So I got into financial technology. After we sold the company, I started working with investment banking firms to buy other technology companies, and they would put me in as a CEO.

We bought a company out of Las Vegas, and I brought headquarters to Utah. So I found myself not only finding opportunities here but then also importing businesses into Utah and expanding our community and our economy here by adding jobs. We built that company up, and I sold that company for $413 million dollars.

I'd become a proven serial tech CEO, and I was also wealthy. I felt like I'd found a secret. I found the pot of gold. I went to work with that, bought another private equity firm, did the same thing. This time it was in Chicago. Again, we established headquarters here, recovered some jobs here, created and grew the company here. And I sold that company for $425 million.

Then I decided that I was going to retire. So I sat on a number of company boards, but then I joined the board of a company called Truckstop.com in Boise, Idaho, and did some financial engineering. We sold that company for $945 million. Oh, wow. I felt like I was on a roll. Then I joined another company here locally in Orem, another financial technology company.

Let me tell you, it's not the money I'm most proud of. It's all companies that I've had association with that I have helped to develop and build our community. We've looked to hire and increase diversity and inclusion.

That's what I love about Weave. We value diversity and inclusion like no other company I've ever seen in the State of Utah. I have 750 plus employees and growing. By the end of this year, we'll have 1,000 employees. I can tell you that in Utah County, I believe Weave is probably one of the most diverse kinds of companies. I don't believe there's another African American CEO in Utah County that is running a billion and a half dollar value company now.

I believe that businesses have a community responsibility to build, strengthen, and nurture through their inclusion of diverse people from all different walks of life and in areas of our society. And so my footprint here in Utah has been huge. I've always tried to let the product of my work speak for my value. I've realized that I've done an injustice to the people that I can inspire and influence. That's what I want to change.

JAMES: *It's very inspiring to hear your story and how you are doing all this in Utah County. There are a lot of Black small business owners, but someone who can create wealth and create jobs on this scale is so important. How do we create more Roy Banks?*

ROY: There are aspiring and budding Black men and women that are trying to make a difference. It's a matter of lifting them up and giving them the support they need.

If you look at the last several years and the social discourse that is taking place in our nation today, we have racial division like we've never seen before. We've got this community strife, this class separation, we've got the socioeconomic division, and the rhetoric that's going on is so, so, so acidic. I'm in Utah and I've been gifted with all of these opportunities. I feel for the first time I actually can have and make a difference. I don't know that I'm ready for public office. I've never really thought about myself as a public servant. I'm a capitalist, there's no doubt about it. But I am looking for some moral or social good, beyond what I've done commercially. I think it's definitely time. How can I help others succeed in a time like this? How can I help bring unity? I'm a CEO that happens to be Black. I'm proud to be Black, and there's no question about it.

JAMES: *So, through your journey, being Black in your county, one of the least diverse in the nation, and growing, what challenges did you have to overcome because of your race?*

ROY: When I was in the service, I was very impressed by some of the women officers, and I'll tell you why. I remember one female officer in particular. I asked her, "So what's it like being a female officer in a branch of service that is predominantly men?" She goes,

CEO Roy Banks at the NYSE announcement of Weave's initial public offering

"I have to be twice as good as a man to earn the same promotion and recognition." Twice as good. Twice as good.

She goes, "If my shoes are twice as bright or shiny as my male counterpart, I'm not good enough." I used to think, *Wow, that sucks*. Yeah, it does. But you know what? It's how I feel. I cannot fail. I don't get the same number of strikes as someone else. I am in an industry where everybody has Ivy League MBAs. It's assumed that I don't even have a degree. The pressure of always being on and watched, always, is incredible in this industry.

At the same time, I lived in New Orleans. My dad is from Texarkana, Texas. Southern racism is very overt. It's very out in the open now. They let you know exactly where they stand. I learned a lot about the ugliness of racism. But sometimes we use that term too easily. What I find here in Utah is there's definitely racism, but there's also a lot of ignorance, man, a lot of ignorance. Like, I moved into a neighborhood in this very affluent neighborhood. We had just emptied the moving truck. This guy walks around the corner, and he goes: "I thought all the blacks lived in West Valley." He's trying to be funny. And I'm thinking, *Is that racist, or is that just ignorant?* It was just ignorant.

When I first started working after I got into the service, I remember leaving my pod and coming back and finding ugly Post-it Notes there. Now that's racist, right? That's a pretty hard thing because, you know, I'm trying to make a living just like everybody else. I'm trying to just do my job and do it well. How many people leave their desk and have to worry about what they're going to find written on their monitor? I'm never not reminded of the struggle that I have had.

The reason I live here is because it's a great place to raise my family. It's been very good to me professionally. And I love the four seasons. There's nothing wrong with Utah to me, but I do feel a sense of challenge that I don't feel when I go to other places that are more diverse now. That's part of why we are working so hard to increase diversity at Weave.

It's not just Utah. It's the industry, too. I go to trade shows, and there's no one that looks like me. No one. And, and my heart hurts because I believe that there should be more. But also, it makes me realize that if I fail, it reflects upon all Black males.

But what I do realize is that I've got big, broad shoulders, and I can carry this weight. And I have overcome, and there have been so many good people that have taken an interest in Roy Banks and wanted to develop me and want to see me be success-ful. They wanted to help me succeed so that others can follow.

> " I have overcome, and there have been so many good people that have taken an interest in Roy Banks and wanted to develop me and want to see me be successful. They wanted to help me succeed so that others can follow. "

> —ROY BANKS

I've been very blessed from the folks who have given me tre-mendous opportunities, with all my other companies to now at the biggest company that I've ever run. But with all this power comes responsibility. That's why I'm doing this. I'm meeting with you right now, and I need to just say this: The work that the Utah Black Chamber is doing is groundbreaking. It's pioneering.

When the president of the NAACP came here, we were talking and he said that we need to *reinvigorate*. I thought it was an interesting word that he used. *Reinvigorate* the influence of Black people in Salt Lake City and their contribution. He did not say "invigorate." He feels like there's an opportunity to have a renaissance of Black impact here. I'm ready to do that.

About three years ago, I had decided to retire. That was until last December, when I started at Weave. For me now, it's starting a new career but with a different purpose and focus.

JAMES: *Tell us about raising your family here and your vision for the future of young Black people.*

ROY: I have six kids, five boys and a girl. My youngest, my daughter, just graduated from high school. So we're out of the graduation years now. So I have three boys in college. I've got two that are married and are working. They all live here in Utah.

We have two grandchildren, and yeah, we've been blessed. My daughter-in-law graduated from BYU, from the J. Reuben Clark Law School, and she's an attorney down in Provo. My two sons are following their father's footsteps. They both work in the tech industry. They're all doing well, and we're very proud of them.

The one thing I can tell you, and I'm always going to, whenever I get a chance to talk about it, we need to teach our children, especially in the Black community, financial literacy, teach them to learn how to use money, learn how to make money work for you, learn the time value of money. If I decide to do something more philanthropic, it will be around financial literacy for Black youth.

I spent twenty years of my career in financial technology. I've worked with companies like payment processors, Visa, Master-Card, Amex, Discover, and all the major banks, Wells Fargo, Zions. I go to trade shows. What's interesting is, if you believe that the financial industry is a microcosm of the white collar world, it's not a good picture of diversity. I could probably count on one hand the number of Black executives I saw working for those financial companies in twenty years. Why are they not pursuing financial jobs and opportunities and education in finance? To me there's something we need to dig down deep into. It's a systemic problem there. People don't get to see people like you and me. We need to make sure that we have places where they can find mentors and see the opportunities. Everybody wants to grow up to be LeBron James, and LeBron James is a fantastic person, man, and athlete. But he represents the smallest percentage of people who actually make it to the big leagues.

He is the 1 percent that get there. But the thing is, the other 99 can do so much more.

An Army aviation maintenance veteran, Alli's first venture stemmed from nearly twenty years of engineering and project management experience. He's worked for several international and Fortune 200 companies and started his first small business, Haight Bey & Associates LLC, in 2014. He won his first Department of Defense contract, worth more than $47 million, the next year. The company has since added several prime and sub contracts to their project portfolio and also has launched a cybersecurity compliance spinoff, Totem Technologies.

JAMES: *So tell us about how your career as an entrepreneur started. What did that look like?*

ALLI: I started Haight Bey out of my basement in 2014, just my wife and I working off an idea that we could capture some defense contracts. We set to work writing proposals. I was subsequently let go from the other defense job I was working, at a Fortune 200 company. They got wind that I had started my own company and didn't like the idea. So in the evenings, I would work as a tortilla line production person for Tyson Foods, as a supervisor. During the day, I'd work up at Snow Basin as a boot, ski, and snowboard technician. So in between technical writing for defense contracts, I was on the slopes or making tortillas. I needed some side hustles so we could put food in the refrigerator and pay rent. We did that for two years. We also took everything we had out of our 401k. We sold a property in Colorado. That gave us a runway to get started. We still have three kids at home, and one of them was in school. All of them were doing extracurricular activities. My wife

Alli Bey in New York for Warrior Rising Annual Board Meeting

is a speech therapist in the school district, so there wasn't a lot of money to be made there.

JAMES: *Wow. And you made it work. So what inspired you to start your own business in the first place?*

ALLI: In 2002, I started working for a company out of Finland, a weather equipment manufacturing company, one of the world's biggest. There, at Viasala, I got handed a tactical Air Force program, and we were building these tactical weather systems and then selling them to the Air Force. Then they would deploy them around the world as they saw fit. So I helped engineer that from the ground up here in the United States. Then they handed me the program, and I started working directly with Raytheon, and

Raytheon was the liaison between the military and the civilian side of the house. So I worked through Raytheon delivering this product to the Air Force. In 2010, the economy had turned pretty bad. Viasala started laying off people here in the United States, and I was on that list. About four months later, I found out that a company here in Utah had won this tactical contract, so I reached out to that company and told them about my experience. They offered me a job, and we moved to Utah with the intent of only being here about four years and then going back to Colorado. Two years into the contract, the government came to the company that I worked for at the time and said, "We no longer can offer this contract as full and open."

In defense contracting terms, you have stuff that's called full and open, and then you have set asides. Full and open means anybody can compete for them, and for set asides, you have to be part of a specific group to bid for these contracts. The one that they set aside for the weather programs was for small business. So my company asked me to go out and find a small business to partner with. I spent about six months trying but couldn't find one that would be willing to partner with us. So I went back to the general manager and said, "I would like to start my own company, and then you can partner with me." They said, "That's a great idea." When I went and did it, though, they fired me on the spot for it. The tricky part is it's an at-will state, so while my general manager thought it was a good idea that I went and started my own company, the legal side of this organization thought that was fraught with disadvantages for the large company that I was working for.

So that's how I ended up in that position, but I knew the contract inside and out. I reached out to all of the equipment manufacturers I've worked with for decades. They agreed to partner with me and gave me pretty advantageous pricing on everything, which afforded my little company the opportunity to win this $50 million contract. I guess it was two years later after starting the company when we were awarded a $47.5 million contract to work this tactical program for the next five years. That took us from 2015 to 2020. Now we just won it again, so we're on the contract now until 2025. It's very lucrative, and it's given us opportunities to help our community and the veteran and minority community around Utah. It's given us the opportunity to grow additional businesses, as well as our secondary company that we've just started called Totem Technologies. Totem Technologies focuses on cybersecurity compliance for small- and medium-sized businesses just like us. So, for small defense contracting companies that are having a hard time proving compliance with cybersecurity standards, we come in and help them out for a fraction of the cost of what the larger managed service providers do it for.

JAMES: *What impact did the pandemic have on your work, especially with a brand new company?*

Alli: It was really hard for us. The management team and I talked about how it was impossible for us to scale because when we first launched the business, the idea was that we were consultants. We would go into organizations and sit with them side-by-side and help them work through all of their cybersecurity policies, procedures, and training material and implement new policies and procedures. So COVID kind of took us by surprise; I honestly thought we were going to have to shut the business down, simply because we couldn't travel and we weren't generating any revenue. My marketing team at the time came up with the idea that we go online, create a virtual classroom, basically. That was a huge dynamic shift for our engineering team because we like to be face-to-face with our clients. We really didn't see an opportunity in going remote or being virtual, but we decided to give it a go. It was probably July or early August of 2020 that we decided that we were going to go online. By the end of the year, we saw that we were so much more scalable and we could keep our staff to a minimum. We could operate from anywhere with online platforms out there, and we found that it was actually easier for us to be online and cheaper for our clients to be online.

We're still getting 100 percent positive feedback for everything that we deliver. That speaks volumes to the team and what we've been able to do. I think it's going to work out where we're probably not going to go back to our original consultative model and instead will remain online. During COVID, we revamped our software, made it so much more user friendly and easier for a non-cyber expert to navigate software in what we call their compliance journey. Instead of hiring new people, we took the revenue and put it into our software or software as a service (SaaS) model. And we're off to the races now with this new recurring SaaS model, doing bigger and better things that we never thought that we would be able to do with a staff of seven.

JAMES: *So it turned out to be better for your business, in terms of scalability. What about Haight Bey, then? Are you looking for additional contracts?*

ALLI: We have multiple contracts. Most center around US Air Force weather, but we do some radio maintenance for different bases around the United States. We've got several construction contracts, we work for the State of Utah, and we're always looking for new opportunities to try out, whether it be at the state, federal, or local level. We've had a few local municipalities reach out, and we help them with cybersecurity concerns or small municipality networks and what we consider critical infrastructure. We help companies identify their weaknesses and flaws in their current cybersecurity policy or even solve problems for issues like water quality. All the water that we drink inside of our homes, all the water that we use for our lawn, all that water flow is monitored by a SCADA system. That's basically an industrial communication protocol that's been around since the 1990s. That's what many municipalities use, and every one of those endpoints is a vulnerability or a way for adversaries to get into our critical infrastructure systems. A lot of municipalities are starting to understand that, and they're asking companies like ours to come in and help them evaluate their infrastructure and figure out where the weak spots are. We can help them harden or shore those up.

JAMES: *I remember taking a tour and seeing the equipment you repair, trying to understand what you do the best I can. You definitely have a lot going on. What also stuck out to me is that, with the big contract you have, it allowed you to give back to the community and allowed you to work with veterans and minorities. Can you tell us what you are doing in that space?*

ALLI: It was probably 2020 and late 2019 when I was working with an organization called Warrior Rising, which basically takes veterans and/or veterans' direct family members and teaches them how to operate or grow a business. So we take veterans and turn them into entrepreneurs, teach them how to fish, so to speak. I came up with the idea that we could take some of these struggling companies that we were helping train and pay their CEO or their startup or their entrepreneur a small salary and give them a place to work and infrastructure, instruction, capability, and access to organizations that have done what they've done before. How fast can we help a company grow and sustain themselves? That was the idea.

So we did a little experiment with a young lady by the name of Trinity Johnson. We brought her company and put them in the incubator space and paid a small salary, so that she didn't have to worry about carrying on a career while she was starting a company. She was successfully able to take her company from about $5,000 annual revenue to over $200,000, just because we were able to insert a little bit of money so that she didn't have to worry about putting food on the table. It was the idea of opening up some of the space that we had in our facility as an incubator space. Right about the same time, I heard about what the Black Chamber was trying to do with setting up a Black Success Center. So working with you guys, we decided that we were just going to combine the two, Warrior Rising into the Black Success Center incubator space, and open that up to any minority or veteran in the business community who needs a space to operate out of with office infrastructure already around it. So some of the private money that we made on that first contract we were able to direct into our veteran and minority communities so they could come in and have a place to grow and develop themselves and their companies.

" So some of the private money that we made on that first contract we were able to direct into our veteran and minority communities so they could come in and have a place to grow and develop themselves and their companies. "

—ALIAHU "ALLI" BEY

Working his way up through the company, Stanton Johnson became president and CEO of Maxam North America and regional director of the company's North and Central America operations. A native of Liberia, he started out at the mining services company, which for years was based in Salt Lake City, in 1990 as a technical services representative. In Utah, he and his family found a place to grow, becoming influential members of Calvary Baptist Church. Now, in retirement, he continues to work as a consultant and has decided to continue to make Utah his permanent home.

JAMES: *I'm excited to have you here because you have grown here in Utah very successfully, but not as a native. You came here from Liberia, correct?*

STANTON: Correct. So we came here about thirty-one years ago now. We were fleeing from a civil war. I graduated from Montana Tech, and then we moved back to Liberia after graduation, and I worked there for about seven years. Then there was a civil war — kind of like what's happening in Afghanistan, right? War broke out. My wife was an American citizen, and all my kids were able to be evacuated. We moved to Tulsa while I was looking for a job. My first interview was in Salt Lake City, Utah. It was 1990. I think it was November. After the interview, I was offered the job, and we've been here since.

JAMES: *Amazing. What was the company?*

STANTON: It was in mining services, and my background is in mining engineering. Basically, I worked with that company all the way

Stanton Johnson

through. The company was acquired by a Spanish company after I had spent ten years there, but it was basically the same organization. I didn't have to leave after the acquisition.

I started off as a technical services representative on the first day. I was responsible for training customers on how to use products and services. Gradually, I got promoted to the operation side, and I was running plants. And then eventually I became responsible for all of our international licensees all over the world.

After that, I was in charge of all of our North American operations: Canada and the United States, parts of South America, and Mexico. I worked several years in that role and then in 2013, I was promoted to the presidency.

JAMES: *Wow. You kept pressing on.*

STANTON: Until I retired in 2017. So it's been a long journey, even before we came here. In Liberia, I used to be superintendent for a mining operation. When we came back to the United States, I said, "Well, the first thing I'm going to do is get help with a search."

And sure enough, I got a headhunter, and my first couple of interviews landed me the job. The Lord is great. We just took off, and we had nothing. So I started my career all over at thirty-five. Looking ahead, it was like we had to start from zero. That in itself was daunting. We had three kids.

JAMES: *Were there any expectations or perceptions you had about moving into Salt Lake?*

STANTON: You know, I didn't have any expectations. My only desire was to work as hard as I could and to support a family, send my kids to school, put a roof over our heads, food on the table, and keep on pressing forward, so I was pretty focused my first several years. When you're Black in a predominantly white culture, in order to excel in that organization, you have to work twice as hard. You have to understand that I had a lot more experience than a lot of folks coming into the company and I was getting resistance, but I wasn't really focused on that because I knew eventually that the work will show for itself, and I tried to ignore all of that difficulty. I couldn't take it too personally because everywhere I went, even as a technical services manager, it was predominantly white: from the mines in Wyoming and Montana to Canada or Tennessee.

" My only desire was to work as hard as I could and to support a family, send my kids to school, put a roof over our heads, food on the table, and keep on pressing forward, so I was pretty focused my first several years. "

—STANTON JOHNSON

I think the reason that I was able to advance was because of my faith. You know, anybody else could have done my job. But they saw that I had certain skills and characteristics like expertise in acid mine drainage and the fact that I was competent enough. I got moved quite a bit and quite rapidly.

One of the things that I became aware of pretty quickly was that as long as I just had a mining engineering degree, I was always going to be looked at as just that technical person who can solve technical problems. So quickly I decided, if I was going to advance in this organization, I have to do something different. I went and got an MBA, and right after I got an MBA, things really started to fall in place for me.

JAMES: *I knew you were president and CEO, but I didn't know it was the same company you started with. You weren't necessarily on the bottom, but you worked all the way up.*

STANTON: Yeah. You know, I basically retired because the company now decided to move the corporate office from Salt Lake City to Dallas, Texas. I was getting too close to retirement to move. I knew this would be a good place and time to retire.

JAMES: *So when you retired, you decided to stay here. You could choose to go anywhere.*

STANTON: My wife and I had some different thoughts. I mean, we bought a place in Arizona, because we thought it would be a place to retire. There's no snow, and the weather is more conducive for eight months in a year. But then, we have family here. We go to church. This is home.

Utah Regional Vice President for Workers Compensation Fund (WCF) Laura Stireman is a change-making corporate leader, volunteer, and board member of the Utah Black Chamber. She has been with WCF Insurance for more than twenty-five years, holding a variety of positions from claims to sales. Currently, she oversees the regional operations for the Agency Relations Department in Utah and the surrounding states. Throughout her career, she has stood out for her dedication, excelling as a mentor, creating training strategies, developing new markets, exceeding goals, and resolving conflicts.

JAMES: *Glad to have you here, not just as part of the Utah Black Chamber but also as a voice representing corporate leadership, particularly in insurance and finance. I don't see a lot of diversity overall in those fields. What do you think the reasons are?*

LAURA: I think it's a couple things. One, those are very old industries, and this is America. Then if you are a young person coming out of college and you're looking for somewhere where you belong, and you don't see anybody who looks like you, it's not attractive. You look at the board, the executive team, and they're all white men. There are not even a lot of women. If I'm just graduating, and I'm looking for a place where I'm going to find a community and some similarities, it's probably not where I go.

I think the tech industry has done a wonderful job of showcasing diversity, and you can find a place there. So I think that's one issue. The second reason is that I think we haven't done a good job in the insurance industry of selling our industry. You hear insurance, and usually you think, *Yeah, no, I don't want insurance.*

Laura speaking with one of her colleagues

I don't like it. It's expensive. But the industry itself offers so much flexibility and so much opportunity. We just need to get out there and sell it.

JAMES: *Well, we certainly appreciate your leadership. What are the next steps for you in your career?*

LAURA: That's an interesting question. Some days I'm like, *No, I'm done.* But I really like what I do. I like where WCF is going. I like what we're doing. I can't see retiring in four or five years; I think I would like to continue at WCF.

JAMES: *Because you're mostly a native here, when it's all said and done and WCF is behind you, do you plan on staying here? Do you think you'll be heading out to Florida with your mom?*

LAURA: I don't know. I really like Utah. It's been a good place. I think we've got a good healthy balance of economic opportunities and quality of life. I feel you can make a good living and have a good life. It would be hard to give up all the space and openness, but then again, it doesn't have a beach.

"I really like Utah. It's been a good place.
I think we've got a good healthy balance of
economic opportunities and quality of life."

—LAURA STIREMAN

JAMES: *Before we wrap up, I want to go back into you moving up through WCF because you pushed through your own limitations when you weren't sure you were ready. Did you feel like, as a person of color, you had to outperform?*

LAURA: I think growing up Black—we call it Black tax—you have to do a little bit more, and I don't know if that's external or internal. It just is. For me, I have felt that we just have to do more to be even. I think some of that comes from being a woman in the industry, too. Of course, nobody ever actually said that, right? I don't know if it's external or internal, but certainly it exists.

JAMES: *Yeah, you know it is the intersectionality that you have as a woman of color, being a woman and Black.*

LAURA: Yes, and there were a few years where I got a lot of feedback about that. I've had to kind of watch my facial expressions and my body language, and I don't know if that's being a woman or being a Black woman.

JAMES: *Well, it's been exciting seeing how bright the future is for Utah, and the efforts that people like you are putting into ensuring that we're becoming more welcoming and investing in the community.*

LAURA: It's been wonderful. I've loved my time at the chamber. It's been fun getting to know everybody and finding another community.

TWO

Community Leadership: Emerging and Veteran Change-Makers

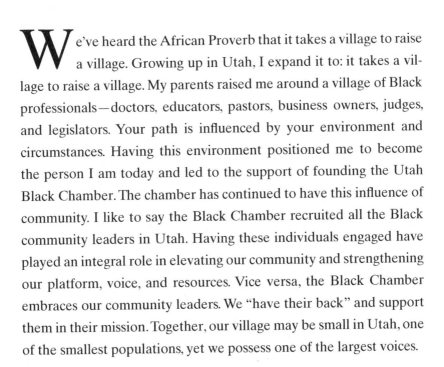

We've heard the African Proverb that it takes a village to raise a village. Growing up in Utah, I expand it to: it takes a village to raise a village. My parents raised me around a village of Black professionals—doctors, educators, pastors, business owners, judges, and legislators. Your path is influenced by your environment and circumstances. Having this environment positioned me to become the person I am today and led to the support of founding the Utah Black Chamber. The chamber has continued to have this influence of community. I like to say the Black Chamber recruited all the Black community leaders in Utah. Having these individuals engaged have played an integral role in elevating our community and strengthening our platform, voice, and resources. Vice versa, the Black Chamber embraces our community leaders. We "have their back" and support them in their mission. Together, our village may be small in Utah, one of the smallest populations, yet we possess one of the largest voices.

This chapter and the next are the strongest chapters, hearing from a few of our community influencers. However, this is just a small sampling of individuals making a significant impact in our community. Utah is fortunate to have people like these who have shared their story here, being pioneers for change and creating and clearing a path for a growing and thriving Black community.

Emma Houston, a Texas native who has lived in Utah since 1986, has built a career based on helping others succeed, from nonprofit work to tackling diversity and inclusion for county government. She is now the Special Assistant to the Vice President of Equity, Diversity and Inclusion at the University of Utah, furthering those same causes and working with students, staff, and faculty. She also works with the university's Black Cultural Center and liaises among different departments and initiatives.

JAMES: *Emma, before we jump into your contributions to the Black community, tell us how you came to be here.*

EMMA: What initially brought us here was that my ex-husband worked for NASA in Florida, and a local company here had been trying to get him to Utah for like three years. We finally said, "Okay, let's just check it out." Of course, they brought us in springtime when the weather was lovely, but we also fell in love with the community and just the environment here in the state of Utah.

When we relocated, I was thinking I can give it five years, tops. More than thirty years later, I'm still here. My oldest daughter lives in South Carolina with her husband, my youngest daughter lives here in Salt Lake City with her husband, my ex-husband is still here as well. But I love Utah. The opportunities here are hand over fist.

Early on, I got involved in the church, NAACP, and the community and just kind of dipped my toe in to see what Utah has to offer for people from my demographics. The population was still what it is now, maybe a percentage has changed just slightly. Utah has sold me on family values, as well as the community as a whole—how we engage, how we can give back, how we can grow and take advantage of opportunities that present themselves. It has been good for me, and good for my career, going into government with Salt Lake County government and now at the University of Utah on a larger scale. The thing that I have learned is that you have got to put yourself in spaces where people get to know who you are. Get to know who holds positions of power in the state of Utah, make those connections, and amplify opportunities for the Black community to advance their careers, their colleagues, their positions, their initiatives.

> " Utah has sold me on family values, as well as the community as a whole—how we engage, how we can give back, how we can grow and take advantage of opportunities that present themselves. "

—EMMA HOUSTON

Although Utah has small demographics as far as ethnicity is concerned, we are very strong in our commitment to what we do and how we help others elevate to the next level. What I have found is a really close-knit community. There are some detractors out there, but still, for the most part, we create a positive atmosphere for individuals, and we want you to be successful. Utah is a great place to raise kids, a great place to establish who you are—if you're an entrepreneur, or if you're starting out new, it really is a great place, but you have to connect yourself and give us some time. When you find your circle, it's very supportive.

Whenever we talk about bringing individuals in, I always say

Emma speaking at the unveiling of
Utah Women's History Memorial

the Divine Nine is in the state of Utah. You know that, right? And
people are surprised that seven of the Divine Nine have alumni
chapters in the state of Utah. When we talk to African Americans, somewhere in their family, they may have that affiliation as
well. Once you connect with a sorority or fraternity, you have a
base in the state of Utah. You have family waiting for you here.
You just have to make the effort to reach out and tell us how we
can help you be successful in this new space.

JAMES: *Talking about being successful, tell us about your story and
how you transitioned to education.*

EMMA: I started out in nonprofits, with the Girl Scouts of Utah for thir-
teen years before transitioning to Salt Lake County government

in aging and adult services. Then I was appointed as director of Diversity Affairs in the mayor's cabinet under Mayor Ben McAdams. Just recently, University of Utah convinced me to come use my talents there. So I'm still doing equity, diversity, and inclusion with the Division of Education and with our Vice President at the University of Utah. So I have had those transitional moves, and they have always elevated me to a higher level and a position of power as well—to the point of being able to be at the University of Utah to craft what equity diversity, inclusion, success, belongingness, and access look like, not only internally for our campus but also externally for our community. What does that partnership look like when you're wanting to send your child to the University of Utah or be an employee at the University of Utah? What type of atmosphere and what type of climate is there? I get to craft that with internal and external audiences.

I've been there since November of 2020, a short time, but already have that deep connection to what is going on. Look at the Black Culture Center. Look at the fact that our former president, Ruth Watkins, during the unrest over this last couple of years, took up the mantle to say we will have a George Floyd Memorial Leadership Academy. We will train leaders from diverse backgrounds to create opportunities, so that when they graduate from the University of Utah they have those skills in place.

We are recognizing that we have populations that have had gaps and identifying what those barriers have been because of systems we have put in place under the leadership of the University of Utah. We are pulling back the curtain. Creating the George Floyd Memorial Leadership Academy is definitely a step in the right direction. We use the Michigan platform as well, and we are training Utah leaders through a lens of equity.

So those two platforms since I have been there are crucial to the work that we do internally on campus and in the community. We are walking the talk. We're not just putting out statements. We're doing the work.

JAMES: *One of the main reasons I was excited to hear about your position is that you've been doing this kind of work, diversity and inclusion, for a long time. You've worked with the government and with big companies. How did you get into it?*

EMMA: One of my mentors was Diane Hesleph. She was a principal here in the state of Utah, and she was doing the work way back when my kids were in high school. She mentored me along the way and introduced me to being a practitioner of equity, diversity, and inclusion. I started that path at Rowland Hall-St. Mark's as their diversity director for new hires and for new students coming on board. They were diversifying their student population as well as their parent population. I have just carried that through all of my career choices, ensuring that we were looking not only through the lens of diversity but also looking into the lens of inclusion and equity as well. It has just elevated up to different levels.

JAMES: *And you also have your own consulting firm, helping build equity strategies, right? What does that look like?*

EMMA: Two other colleagues and I have been working with Utah Highway Patrol. We started last June, because one of the lieutenants said we need to have a deep-dive conversation, and we need to have a different perspective and lived experiences. So we have had that one-on-one training with over four hundred Utah highway patrolmen. We are on Phase Two now. They have heard the conversation, they have provided input, and so now we're looking at *what now*. The why. *Let's talk about how you're going to change and how you're going to live out your mission to serve and protect all communities.* What is that going to look like through a lens of equity?

JAMES: *You mention diversity, equity, and inclusion—and people usually just focus on those three—but you also keep adding in belonging. Why?*

EMMA: When we're talking about inclusion, we're saying that all of us in the room have a voice—that our thoughts, our opinions, our perspective, our lived experiences are valid, and that we can express that. Belonging means that I have the opportunity to elevate my career as well, that I am seen as leadership potential, that I am mentored, that I am coached, that I am sponsored, that I am part of the overall organization. And it cannot just be because of my perspective, but also because I can bring value to the organization, and I belong in this space. That is different for each individual. What belonging means to you is going to be totally different than what belonging means to me. So how do we create that space where my thoughts, my opinions, my lived experience are part of the conversation?

One of the things that individuals from different backgrounds don't want to be is that token person. So when leaders are saying that you belong here, it's because the leaders understand your lived experience, you are a part of the conversation, you are part of our organization, and you belong here—not just because of your skin tone or your language but because you bring value to what we are doing.

What leaders should consider is: *Have I built a relationship with that individual?* And do I understand what their skills are, what their lived experiences are, and how they contribute to the success of our organization, or corporation, or our business? Once we have that relationship in place, then we're looking at that person as contributing to the success of the organization, not because they look a certain way but because they have the skills and the talents and the abilities to help drive this organization to the next level. It's about building relationships and understanding how those relationships can expand the work that you're doing.

With more than forty years as a change agent in the City of Ogden and in Utah, Betty Sawyer has held many titles: chair of Diversity Affairs for the city, recently retired community engagement coordinator in Access & Diversity at Weber State University, and member of the US Civil Rights Commission's Utah Advisory Council, to name a few. She is also a past president of the Ogden NAACP, a charter member of the Greater Salt Lake Alumnae Chapter of Delta Sigma Theta Sorority Inc., and co-founder of the grassroots nonprofit Project Success Coalition. She also has been and continues to be a champion for Juneteenth celebrations across the state.

JAMES: *You've clearly been an active player in the Utah Black community—in ways that would be hard to capture in one go. Could you start with telling us how you ended up in Utah in the first place?*

BETTY: My oldest brother, Will, lived here. He was traveling from Long Beach with some friends and they said, *Oh, stop in Utah.* He did, and he fell in love with the mountains and the great outdoors.

I'm from Maryland, the beach, the Atlantic Ocean. I graduated in 1975 from Morgan State University in Baltimore and, just like any other event in the family, it was a huge family reunion. Relatives came from North Carolina and Virginia. One of my aunts was graduating in Baltimore as well. So we all converged together after graduations for the meal, and during that conversation, one of my siblings—I don't recall who it was, and no one owns up to it—had this great idea to go back to my grandfather's farm in North Carolina one more time.

Betty with youth volunteers of the NAACP Ogden Chapter

My grandfather was a farmer and a longshoreman in Nor-folk, Virginia. Everybody said, "Okay, sounds fun." A week later, May 30, my grandfather passed away. Instead of everybody going to North Carolina for this other celebration, we were there for a homegoing celebration. My oldest brother, Will, came in from Utah, in a Winnebago, to the funeral. In a matter of two weeks, he had talked my brother-in-law and four or five other guys into getting into this Winnebago with him and going to this place un-known.

My sister pulled out an encyclopedia for me to show me Utah. *Oh, it's close to California.* I had just graduated, didn't have a job. It looked close to California—so Utah, what the heck. The men came out first, and then three months later, got settled, found jobs, all of that fun stuff. I traveled with my sister and her brand new child to Utah in the seventies. I remember so distinctly coming into Utah.

I said, "Oh, my goodness." It's like seven o'clock on a Sunday. Everything was shut down. I got up the next day to see what Utah really looked like. I'm looking for Black people. I didn't see Black people the first day, or the second day. It took me two weeks to see Black people in downtown Salt Lake. I thought there has to be a community someplace, but where is it? After that two weeks, I was at the grocery store with my sister, and we saw a Black lady, Mary Green.

She says, "Come to my church." That was Calvary. Growing up where I did, with my mom and NAACP and church and all of that, you come to a new place and you know to look for the church and NAACP. That was tradition. She invited us to Calvary, opened those doors, and it was like heaven. *Okay, Utah might be okay after all.*

JAMES: *So your brother fell in love with the mountains. He dragged you guys out here. Were you staying here just for him? Or was there something else that was drawing you into Utah?*

BETTY: My brother had a plant shop as well. He's been a vegetarian and vegan for forever, so we worked in his plant shop and then got to meet a few people and saw the yuppie side of Salt Lake City. That's a cool vibe.

I decided to go check out the college, thinking maybe I'll look into going to grad school. My major is physical education with a minor in physical therapy. So I called up to the U of U and made an appointment with the advisor for health sciences and had a meeting with him. We sat down to talk for about a half an hour, and at the end of the meeting, he offered me a job.

They had a physical therapy school there, a bachelor's program, but it would require me going back to school for two years. And that area had potential, but when he offered me the job, I said, *Oh, yeah, I could do Utah a little longer. Winter's coming; I'll hang out.* And so I started working at the university as a minority health sciences recruiter and was there for two years doing that work. The next year, I got into the physical therapy school, and boom, boom, boom.

JAMES: *You've been in education for a while. You just retired from Weber State University. What were you doing there?*

BETTY: I was in community engagement. Well, I had a couple different roles. I did direct their Gear Up programs, gaining early awareness and readiness for undergraduate programs. I directed their Ogden City partnership and their state partnership and then saw an opportunity to do grant work. I was doing that on the side for my nonprofit. Then I moved into community engagement, developing partnerships on and off campus. And then I did some student advisement as well and ended up advising our Black Student Union and establishing our Weber State University NAACP Chapter.

JAMES: *So what was it that inspired you to switch from health sciences to community engagement?*

BETTY: I was always in the community. I was a civil rights activist, NAACP president, PTA president. I'm the youngest daughter in my family and my mom, Miss Katherine Walston, was always a community person. That's what she did. She loved young people. Our house was open to any and everybody my entire life. You could be a stranger and walk in and get a meal; that's just the way it was. They were so old school, and they took us wherever they went. For seven days a week, you were going to be at church.

Seven days a week, you were at the NAACP meeting, waiting for the meeting to be over, sitting in the corner, reading your book or doing whatever. My mom opened the first food pantry in our community to respond to a need. She rallied to get a playground built in our section of the community.

So activism was a part of me, starting in college. I got involved politically, working on campaigns, mainly stuffing envelopes, making phone calls, that kind of thing. Activism was always a part of me, and coming here looking for a church and the NAACP—two things I knew—I continued that work.

> " Activism was always a part of me, and coming here looking for a church and the NAACP— two things I knew—I continued that work. "

—BETTY SAWYER

I skipped the part about getting married along the way. That was what landed me in Ogden. Another part of my story is the days on the basketball court. Like I said, I was fresh out of college where I'd been playing, lettering in all sports, team captain, all of that kind of fun stuff. And my brother is a basketball player, and he has a wicked skyhook that he taught me.

JAMES: *That's a forgotten skill these days.*

BETTY: Yeah, I spent probably ten years in Salt Lake and Ogden, playing with all the sisters and some of our Latina sisters. We had softball teams that were wicked. We played volleyball, all of that.

I spent a lot of time at Central City and Liberty Park playing basketball with the fellas. I would be the ringer until they caught on, and I could really play.

So I met Rich Sawyer, my brother-in-law, on the basketball court. He told me, "You've got to meet my brother." I was like, "I'm good." Eventually, though, an Earth, Wind & Fire concert is where I first met my husband, at what's now the Salt Palace. Rich said, "This is my brother Mike." A couple days later, I was at Liberty Park. That was the other thing we did—in Salt Lake, you would cruise the park, especially Sunday after church. Get some food, turn the music up. And so they come riding through. My friend from Chicago is like, "Stop them, I'm trying to move." I flagged him down and talked him into helping my friend move. After that, I felt guilty when he asked me for my number, so I gave him compensation. He *did* work hard.

This might be year forty-five of marriage for us. I stopped counting. We have four kids and twelve grandchildren who are such a joy.

JAMES: *You mentioned that you moved to Utah thinking California is just around the corner. How often did you visit when you first got here?*

BETTY: Almost immediately. I got to put my feet in the other ocean. Everyone was willing to go and free enough—that's one of the things I think that felt good about Utah, that free spirit. My brother was out in the woods, in the desert, going camping—things I had not done before, but almost every weekend, we were out someplace exploring. It was wonderful. Our kids grew up on that as well. The first vehicle I purchased in Utah was a van for that purpose. I got hooked on going places.

*Betty at the Capitol with Rep. Sandra Hollins and
Project Success Coalition volunteers*

JAMES: *We have an amazing landscape for that outdoor experience,
and we want to promote that more to the Black community. But
fast-forward for us now. When people think of Juneteenth in Utah,
of course they're going to think of Miss Betty Sawyer. Share with
us the journey of what got you started here.*

BETTY: As you know, I served as director of the Governor's Office
of Black Affairs for almost ten years. All kinds of experiences
came along with it. It was a wonderful journey, opening doors of
opportunity for our community.

So when I heard about Juneteenth, Louis, Bush, Minnesota,
my buddy—rest in paradise—he invited me over to Utah Indus-
trialization Center, which was a job training program. Murphy,
Gail, Ortega, my buddy from Baltimore, Greg, they were all at the
center, and they were talking about Juneteenth.

So I'm like, *What is it?* They told me to come on out. The first one I went to was over at Jordan Park. I think it was 1988. It was a picnic. They had music, folks singing and dancing. A baseball game.

So when the next year rolled around, I was invited to participate in the planning committee. We had been meeting, making all of these wonderful plans for Juneteenth, and I came to one of the meetings and found out that the folks responsible for reserving the park had not done it. It was like two weeks away, unfortunately. We thought we'd have to cancel. So I said, "Let me make some calls." I had a buddy in Ogden that runs the community center, and it has a big park attached to it. So I called Maurice White and said, "We need help. We've got to have somewhere to have this festival." He says, "Come on up."

It went so well, even with a two-week notice, even in terms of some of the regulations for parks, having music and vendors and all of that. We said, "Let's keep doing it up in Ogden.:" We could really do something here. That was my introduction.

A part of my commitment was to make sure that we expanded that and had something in Salt Lake and Ogden to bring the community together. From that point on, in 1989, I continued to promote the holiday and tried to work with folks to keep it alive. We just made it happen in both communities.

JAMES: *What keeps you wanting to do it?*

BETTY: The fact that it is important in itself. It's another one of those stories that we don't all know a lot about. I run into people even today who don't know what Juneteenth is. I'm from Maryland, and we didn't have Juneteenth. And we had Frederick Douglass, Harriet Tubman—all of those folks born and raised and coming up through that area. I have a lot of people from Texas, and that's how it ended up being celebrated here in Salt Lake, in Ogden.

I felt it was important to continue to build that legacy. I fought for about twelve years trying to make it a holiday. I've been serving on the National Board of the Juneteenth Observance Foundation for over twenty years. That was one of our major agenda items. How do you institutionalize these things, so that they have life beyond us? So our kids and their kids will have an opportunity to know and experience it? I've had good support. It was one of the things we were able to get the governor to support, and then some of our local industries. We just sent out a call and said, "Whoever wants to come to the table to help plan the event, you're welcome to do that." And we continue to try to move forward.

One of the things that we saw with the Black Lives Matter movement and George Floyd was this heightened awareness of Juneteenth and more and more people wanting to celebrate. So I think, even this year, we probably have twenty Juneteenth celebrations going on someplace. Our goal is to have as many people who are willing to come in a unified effort, because I think that's one of the things that we have to constantly remind ourselves of as Black people in Utah. You can forget sometimes—just moving in and doing what you have to do—the importance of building community and maintaining community. It's still there because that's our DNA.

It's now a holiday in Utah. [Former] Governor Herbert and Sandra Hollins and Senator Alvin Jackson—we were able to get them to sponsor it. Now how do we build on that to create those legacies in other areas? Everyone from chambers to working with the museum to be able to tell our story?

And how do we really make it become that statewide event? Just recently, the Utah Board of Higher Education passed a resolution encouraging all of the systems of higher education institutions to honor, promote, and celebrate Juneteenth. I got a call from a mutual friend at Utah State who connected me, and they're doing an event. So we've been working with Utah State for the last month or so helping them plan.

Over the years, in our partnership with Weber State, even before I worked there, we had held gym teams and had great stuff going on. I said let's use it. When I worked at the U of U, we had a Juneteenth celebration there; I was able to get our Black Student Union together. Salt Lake Community College—Miss Glory— we've done some things with her for Juneteenth, and Ogden Weber Applied Technology, they've been one of our sponsors off and on for about ten years, doing the Juneteenth celebration. So we've really taken it statewide, but always having synergy in what we do. One of the things that we fought to make sure is that all of us weren't trying to do it on June the 19th. God got a month all in twenty-eight days, and with our community, we can do something the whole month. Matter of fact, let's do something all year. And let's take turns instead of having twenty events in two days. We want to support each other and have the economic impact we want. Even more so, we want to do that community building.

You being with the chamber, one of the things that I continue to challenge is the notion of wealth building. How do you build wealth if you have to start from zero every time? That doesn't happen. It doesn't happen. So why do you want to start from zero even in events? Let's build upon what we have. If you're doing this event, let's work with you to expand it because there's plenty of space for all of us to come together.

If you don't like that, let's see how we can change it to make it work. Or again, spread it out so that we can all reap the benefit and our kids can reap the benefit. We can leverage that support economically to do those bigger things that we know we need and want to do.

THREE

Community Leadership: Shaping Law & Policy in Utah and Beyond

A champion for minorities, Utah State Rep. Sandra Hollins was the first African American woman to serve in the Utah State Legislature. For six years and counting, she's represented the people of District 23 and beyond as a leader in the broader Black community. Among other battles, she fought and won a measure to have slavery taken out of the state's constitution, a cause she's now taking up in other states. She and her husband moved to Utah thirty years ago, and she wouldn't trade her lifestyle or opportunities for any other place.

JAMES: *Representative Sandra Hollins, the first African American woman in Utah State Legislature. What do you think about when you hear that?*

REP. HOLLINS: You know, an African American senior citizen came up to me a couple weeks after I won the election, and she said to me: "I stayed up all night. I could not go to sleep until I heard the result of your election. Afterwards, I cried, because I never thought that I would live to see a Black woman walk onto the House floor of the Utah State Legislature."

Wow. I teared up. I realized the impact. A lot of our senior citizens, this is what they worked so hard for. I realize that I am the result of all of the hard work they put in and the road they paved, and I'm pretty much standing on their shoulders right now. It's an honor and a privilege that I never want to take for granted. But it's a lot. It is a heavy burden, because I realized that I not only represent District 23 but also a lot of the Black community. I have a lot of people in my community who say to me, "I don't care who is over my district, you're my representative. You're the person that I feel comfortable talking to, the person I feel understands me and my point of view." I'm the person that they call. I hear everything that's going on in the community, and I'm the person that they trust with their dreams of what they want Utah to be. It's a heavy load, but it's a good load, and it's an honor to be able to carry it.

JAMES: *How have recent national events impacted your role? How have things changed after the murder of George Floyd?*

REP. HOLLINS: I watched the video like everybody else and sat there with disbelief as this man was being murdered. I knew it was going to have an impact on Utah, because we have a lot of people out there who are already fighting for change, who are very passionate about social justice issues and reform. So when all of the civil unrest happened, I started calling my colleagues up, the minority caucus people, and we knew that we had to speak out. We had to say something, because our communities were depending on us to lead. I called for peaceful protests, and I met with a lot of the young people in our community. I think I have a pretty good pulse on what's happening; I try to give voice to our community. I was prepared to take the lead on this. Then the Speaker of the House also stated that he wanted me to take the lead on this, and I am grateful that they recognize that there was a need for me to be at the front of this.

I was happy to do that, happy to help sponsor legislation and policy to try to make change. I'm happy to sit down and listen, so I can try to bridge that gap between the people who are out there on the frontline protesting and our legislators. I try to help them understand where these young people are coming from, why they want change, and what their issues are. I'm also helping young people to understand how we go about making change, to show them how policy is done. I'm happy to be able to provide that bridge.

JAMES: *I appreciate that. It does seem to me that the Utah Legislature operates a little more cohesively than a lot of other states, especially other conservative states. Is there a lot of working across party lines?*

REP. HOLLINS: There are a lot of things we're not gonna agree on because we have different ideologies, but for the most part, behind the scenes, we all get along pretty well. We have lunch together, we have dinner together, we go to each other's kids' weddings. But there's also a lot of education that goes on behind the scenes. There's a lot of me explaining why I feel the way I feel in my lived experience, and there's a lot of me understanding why individuals feel the way they feel, and *their* lived experience. And I think that's where we come together. That's where we try to create policy that is good for the entire community. Of course, there are some things I'm always against, but I think for the most part, we try to work together and come up with policy that's going to be good for the state.

JAMES: *And you've been able to make meaningful change. If you were to name the top three biggest accomplishments, what would they be?*

REP. HOLLINS: Number one would be when I took slavery out of Utah State Constitution. Then when I made the bill banning "knee on the neck" as a form of restraint by law enforcement— that was important. And then when I passed legislation around the school-to-prison pipeline, helping to keep kids out of that.

JAMES: *Share with me how that policy works?*

REP. HOLLINS: The policy that I wrote requires our Student Resource Officers in the schools to have training when it comes to working with kids from different cultural backgrounds and also when working with kids that may have different mental health issues.

Studies have shown that when kids are in contact with law enforcement, and the more they have contact with them, the more likely they are to be suspended—and the more likely they are to be suspended, the more likely they are to go into the school-to-prison pipeline.

Overwhelmingly in the State of Utah, our Native American children are being targeted, or being funneled into the pipeline, and also particularly kids of color. The bill says: Let's have this cultural training so you know how to work with our kids, so you have a better understanding of them. Let's come up with some other measures to be able to discipline our kids so that they will not enter suspension and an arrest won't be an option. What can we set in place other than suspension and arrest?

JAMES: *Has there been discussion about pulling resource officers out of schools?*

REP. HOLLINS: Student Resource Officers are going to be in our school; that's the reality. There is no appetite in the State of Utah to remove them. So what I propose we do is find ways to make sure that they're well trained. How do we better define their roles in the school system? How do we go about making sure that while they're in schools, the interactions with our kids are appropriate? How do we make sure there are resources in the school for our kids who may be experiencing trauma and may need somebody to talk to?

I have met some SRO roles who have turned out to be mentors for our kids, and some of those kids, as a result, have wanted to go into law enforcement. They have seen what those officers can do and how they can make a difference. If they're going to be in our school system, the best thing is to define their role and make sure that they are playing a positive role in the system.

JAMES: *Going back to the other accomplishments, tell us about getting slavery out of the state constitution. That was 2019? How is that even possible?*

REP. HOLLINS: During the time Utah was trying to become a state, my understanding is they tried to mimic as much of the United States Constitution as they could, to be accepted. Part of that was the Thirteenth Amendment. This was after the Emancipation Proclamation, and what it says is that "if you are duly convicted of a crime," you can be placed back into servitude. That happened for economic reasons, because after slavery ended, all of a sudden, you have all of these industries—cotton and all these other industries—trying to figure out how they're going to get free labor. Then they developed what was called Black codes, which meant that they could arrest you for any reason. So you and I are sitting here having this conversation on the street, they can decide we're loitering—and they can arrest us, place us into prison, and then lease us out to these different organizations or these different companies to work. That's how they ended up still being able to maintain free labor. And that was the beginning of the mass incarceration of Black men.

The thing is, we're not the only state. I'm working on the national level, trying to pull this language out of not only other state constitutions, but also the Thirteenth Amendment. Our goal is to change that.

" I'm working on the national level, trying to pull this language out of not only other state constitutions, but also the Thirteenth Amendment. Our goal is to change that. "

—SANDRA HOLLINS

JAMES: *Finally. Here we are, in 2021. Thank you for your work to make change, not only on the state level but also across state lines. Switching topics a little bit, you've been able to rise up and take the lead after living here for many years and raising a family here. What do you feel people are missing about the Utah experience, particularly the African American experience here?*

REP. HOLLINS: My husband and I, we've been here for thirty years. I came from New Orleans, and I'm originally from Cleveland, Mississippi. It has not always been easy. One thing I can say is that hanging in there and staying here has worked. It has definitely been worth it.

During the recession, my husband and I were able to ride it out without getting behind on our mortgage, without suffering economically, because Utah is a good state to live in for that. We've never had any problems finding or maintaining jobs while we were here. The problems we've had, we've learned how to work through them and how to look at the big picture of why we're here. Utah is a good state to live in if you're a minority; it's just a lot of finding your niche, finding people to support you, finding people to talk to who are going to help you navigate. I think the key is finding mentors.

JAMES: *You just said a lot of what I always try to preach about. Other than the economy, what else do you enjoy about Utah?*

REP. HOLLINS: I enjoy the fact that we have downtown, and I love where I live: the west side of Salt Lake City. I love that I'm near downtown but I can also go to the mountains if I want to get away for a while. I love that I'm near Vegas if I want to run off for the weekend. I love the fact that in Utah, a lot of the Black community was so small that we know everybody. If you need something, there's somebody in the Black community that you can find. Everybody knows everybody. You know, my daughters didn't always have an easy time here, but for the most part, I felt that they were safe growing up here. I love the fact that they have friends from all different cultural backgrounds and experiences. Having friends from different backgrounds and economic status adds value to their experience and to their knowledge, and they've learned skills that they can take into the workforce. I tell everybody, my daughters can go from the hood to the White House, and they will be comfortable in any of those situations.

JAMES: *It's true that you can be in one neighborhood here and have every economic status.*

REP. HOLLINS: My daughters were raised with people who have high school diplomas and people who have PhDs, and they all played significant roles in their lives. They're comfortable around everyone. If you think about it, that's the way the Black community has always been. I remember when I took a tour of Martin Luther King's home in Georgia, and one of the things the tour guide was talking about was how in this community you have the doctors and teachers, but you also have the custodians, the waiters, and

Representative Hollins speaking at the Capitol with support from
Rev. Dr. France Davis and wife, Willene and grandson, behind her

the waitresses—all of these people in one community. Our kids knew all of these people with all these wonderful backgrounds and all these wonderful stories in this one community. I think everybody has a story to share and a lesson to teach.

JAMES: *So, you've lived here in Utah. You've run successfully for public office three times now in this state. You went to DC for President Obama's inauguration. You've now had the chance to meet with the first Black Asian vice president. What was that like?*

REP. HOLLINS: That was an awesome, awesome experience. I had a chance to sit on the floor and listen to the debate, and then I had a chance to go to the airport as she was leaving and have a few words with her. She said something that was very powerful and profound: "Just remember, when you stand in that room, you may be the only Black woman—but we're all standing there with you." So every Black woman who is the "first of," we feel like we are all standing there with her. It just gives me chills. That will always stick with me.

JAMES: *That's a big responsibility, too. It feels like we're not just carrying ourselves as Sandra Hollins or James Jackson but also as a Black person in Utah. As you've said, it also comes with a lot of opportunity, too. Opportunity and responsibility. Looking ahead, what are some of the things you hope to change here, in your role as a leader?*

REP. HOLLINS: I'm working on getting more people up in the capitol. That's Number One. I'm always looking at who I can bring in. When I step out, who is going to step into my shoes? I'm also continuing to work on issues around the school-to-prison pipeline. I'm working on issues around law enforcement and police reform. I've been brought into a conversation around Utah's foster care system.

JAMES: *What is the next step for you?*

REP. HOLLINS: I've always said that when I no longer feel the passion, then it's time for me to let somebody else come up. I think the thing that keeps me going is knowing that we can make changes in this community, and that I can be part of that change, that there are people out there who are willing to stand with me and fight with me.

There are still the things that keep you up at night. *What could I have done better? What should I have done or said, or could I have made a difference in this area?* A lot of times people say I make some of the most passionate speeches on the House floor. I don't ever plan on speaking. For the most part, I'm quiet on the floor. But if something strikes me, if I think, *This is wrong*, or *This is going to have a negative impact on a marginalized community, the Black community, or whoever*, there's that fight. I won't go out until something is done. That is just part of the passion. It's just there. I don't know if it's ever going to go away. I always said that if I step out of office, I'm going to probably move more to an activist role.

JAMES: *Instead of stepping back, have you ever thought about stepping up from the House to the role of Senator, or Governor?*

REP. HOLLINS: I've learned to not say no. I am open to whatever God has next for me. That's a safe way of putting it. That's not something I'm looking at, but if doors open, and if God leads me in that direction, then that is where I'm going.

JEANETTA WILLIAMS

Jeanetta Williams is president of the NAACP Salt Lake Branch and NAACP Tri-State Conference of Idaho, Nevada, and Utah. She's also a former member of the NAACP National Board of Directors and a former member of the Utah State Bar Ethics and Discipline Committee, investigating grievances against lawyers. She's a powerful force in legislative and community issues locally, statewide, and nationally.

JAMES: *So what inspired you to activism on this level? How did you become president of the Utah NAACP Chapter?*

JEANETTA: Well, I was president for the Salt Lake branch and went on to become president for Idaho, Nevada, and Utah. One of the reasons is really because they were looking for leadership. I thought, well, let me put my hat in. Because of all the things that I was doing and my background, I felt that I was very qualified, so I ran and was elected. Even after that, I served on the National Board of Directors, which is no longer national. My term was from 1996 to 2002. I still serve on a lot of the national committees. I work very closely with that chairman of the board, Leon Russell, and present CEO Derek Johnson. I've worked with our legal folks, the folks at Nashville, and a lot of the staff. It's more hours than people realize. For instance, we just had our resolutions committee meeting about three weeks ago, and we started at seven o'clock in the morning and went until six o'clock at night with an hour break for lunch. That was on a Thursday. Then the same on Friday. Then Saturday morning was the same thing, except we ended around noon.

Now, how in the world would you ever do that with a full-time job? I couldn't do it. I retired in 2010. Before the pandemic,

Representative Sandra Hollins accepting a NAACP
Award from President Jeanetta Williams

we would be in person, and it would be in Baltimore, so before
I retired, I would take my own personal vacation time to go to
conventions and meetings. That was how strongly I felt about the
work of the NAACP.

JAMES: *What are some of the top things that you've been able to accomplish here in Utah as president of NAACP?*

JEANETTA: One of the things I'm most proud of is Dr. Martin Luther
King Jr. Day. Years ago, it was called the Utah Human Rights
Day. I looked for some sponsors and co-sponsors, but I couldn't
find many. Finally, I was able to find sponsors and get that bill
passed during the 2000 Utah Legislative Session. That was a lot
of work because so many people were saying, "why do we want
to do that?" Or "Dr. King was never here." I personally carried a
letter to the president of the LDS Church. The president and their
board of directors had delivered a letter to me during legislative

session, and they voted to support that bill. In 1992, I was able to get Mrs. Rosa Parks to come to Utah. She presented our very first Rosa Parks award to Mary Green. I spent days and nights talking with her in her hotel room and took her to visit and speak at the University of Utah, and down to BYU. After she passed, I took it upon myself to start working to get some streets named after her in Salt Lake City, West Jordan, and West Valley City—also a bench in Sandy, Utah.

JAMES: *That's amazing. Thank you. I didn't even know about the different Rosa Parks streets. You've been able to connect with some incredible people here in Utah to get the work done. Who have you been most excited to be able to meet with and talk to?*

JEANETTA: Well, one of the people that I was most excited about meeting—I did meet President Clinton and his wife—but the person that I was most very most influenced by who I met and talked to was President Nelson Mandela in the White House. They invited me to a ceremony in the garden area, and we were with the Congressional Black Caucus. I got to talk with him.

JAMES: *What was that conversation?*

JEANETTA: It was good. I introduced myself, told him who I was, and the NAACP, and he even had a tear down his eye. He said, "I so much admire the work of the NAACP." And then he told me, "You know, our ANC [African National Congress] was modeled after the NAACP."

JAMES: *That's great. Since you brought it up, who have you been most excited to work with and talk to in Utah?*

JEANETTA: There have been a few people that were really good for me to work with. One was President Gordon Hinckley, former president of The Church of Jesus Christ of Latter-day Saints. He was always not just interested in what was going on in the church, but also in the community. He was always interested in how folks were treating us. People probably didn't know that much about him, but every time he would see me, he would always make sure that he let me know that if there's anything whatsoever that I need, I should let him know and he'll get it taken care of.

JAMES: *I think people have misconceptions about the LDS Church. Yes, I mean, at one time, and maybe even in some ways now, they do dominate the culture here. But they do work hard to be a welcoming place.*

JEANETTA: I think a lot of people don't really understand what they are trying to do. A lot of people ask me whether they have tried to get me to join the church. Well, they haven't. They *have* been interested in the welfare of the community.

JAMES: *Building on the work that we do at organizations like the Utah Black Chamber and the work the NAACP is doing, we are finally having conversations about issues like Black Lives Matter Utah on a broader scale. People like you are doing this work to make Utah a better place. Can you talk to us about what keeps you going and what keeps you here?*

JEANETTA: It's like my pastor, Pastor Corey Hodges, said yesterday: God sent you here for a reason. And that's what he was telling everybody in the church. People think, *Why Utah, of all places?* I mean, I could be doing this same work in Atlanta, or in any other place. But I chose to stay here in Utah because I felt that there was work to be done. I just think there's so much potential here in Utah, and for the most part, people want to work together. They want to see progress and see things get done.

" I just think there's so much potential here in Utah, and for the most part, people want to work together. They want to see progress and see things get done. "

—JEANETTA WILLIAMS

Sometimes it might take several meetings for even our elected officials to really get it—and that's one of the things I've been doing lately, too, is holding meetings with officials in Congress and our senators to hold them accountable. They are there not only for the white community, but they're there for the communities of color, too.

We're saying that we don't want just a spot at the table, we want to have a voice at the table. So we want to make sure that we

Jeanetta Williams with Betty Sawyer, Rep. Hollins and education leaders

can do that. That voice—the collective voice of NAACP or others from our community—[elected officials] need to know that we are concerned about all of these issues: voter suppression, church floor policing, Black Lives Matter. white lives matter, but we're saying Black lives matter because it's Black people who are getting killed. Look at Sandra Bland; she ended up dead, and then they want to say it's suicide. So what I'm saying is we have a lot to fight. A lot of those happened in other states, but when we talk about NAACP, we're all one big group. Addressing this on a broader scale is going to help everybody.

JAMES: *You've been retired for over eleven years, and you're still just as engaged in this work as you ever were. What inspires you to keep moving after retirement?*

JEANETTA: I think it's just the different subjects that come up. I guess they call me a news junkie, because I'm always looking at the news, I get alerts on my phone. I look to see if it's happened here in Utah, and then see how we can respond, no matter when it happens. I might do a press release if I can't get to the media, if it's late at night. That's what happened with the Pride flag down in Kaysville. I had to send a note on that one saying we denounce all the different hate acts, and I had to do it immediately. We're out there not only just fighting for what's going on in the Black community but also in all communities.

FOUR

Small Business Leadership

O ver the last decade, Utah has been ranked at the top in the United States as the best place to start a business. Utah prides itself in becoming a business-producing machine with many accessible resources, one of the most diverse economies, and business-friendly laws to bring any business idea to life and provide an environment for success. Although the pandemic caused many businesses to suffer and shut down, even harsher for the Black community, we began to see more new businesses established in 2021. While this environment holds true for the majority of the small businesses here, how about the Black small businesses? How equipped is Utah to help the diverse small businesses? It's one of the main reasons the Black Chamber was founded. It saw a need to help the Black business community not only understand the resources available but also build the bridge of understanding and connection so the Black businesses find comfort and support within these resources. The Black business community itself is also very diverse. While we still have our barbershops, salons, and food service businesses, we also have businesses from therapists, collection agencies, and education technology companies. Utah is positioned and poised to elevate Black businesses like it has never before.

Since the beginning, the main challenge the Black Chamber and community has had is identifying Black small businesses. Businesses have the option to identify themselves as minority-owned when they register with the department of commerce, but few do so. And with the Black community the smallest in Utah, it becomes even more challenging. The first Black Chamber event consisted of mainly church friends and family, and not many businesses. The hope was people would spread the word and small businesses would come around. We began with a small list, and grew incrementally.

When we began growing our membership, our main agenda was bringing visibility to these businesses, not just to the Black community but to all of Utah, introducing them to the general community, and seeking opportunities for them to become vendors for large corporations. The importance of this increased more significantly during the Black Lives Matter movement in 2020. People and companies were constantly contacting the Black Chamber to learn how they can support and "Buy Black." Not all of our members are Black-owned businesses. We have large corporate members, nonprofits, and individuals as active members as well. Becoming a member of the chamber is becoming a member of the Black economy—you're seeking to connect, learn, and grow, but also support by providing resources, education, and a platform. Thus, when scrolling through our chamber directory, one is not able to identify which business is Black-owned. Ultimately, our goal is not only being the voice for Utah's Black businesses but also to have all Black businesses as members of the chamber. Later in the summer of 2020, in partnership with one of the tech companies, we launched a Black business directory for Utah.*

---

* www.utahblackpages.com

This is a free directory for Black small businesses to list their business, and people can access this page and look for businesses to support. One of our corporate members used this page for gift baskets to send to their employees who have been working remotely during COVID to boost employee morale. Other corporations use the page to seek restaurants and caterers. The Black Pages creates a foundation of our mission to increase visibility to Black-owned businesses. A community as small as the Black community in Utah, and spread throughout the valley, Black businesses can't survive with just support from the Black community. It takes a village to raise a village. We all need each other to survive, and by creating bridges of understanding, connection, and access, our communities will not only survive but thrive.

The chamber also worked to identify the business resources in the community to support our members. We created a committee of these resources that works to identify how to bring their resources into our membership. One of the great aspects of the Utah business culture is collaboration. We compete with each other, but as a state, we want to be the best and lift each other up. I call it "coopertition." To be the best, you want to beat the best. That's what I have seen here in Utah. In our chamber committee of resources, the thought came to develop an online program to better connect business owners to various resources. Utah has so many resources for small businesses, but it's still a challenge at times to know and understand where they are and how they support small businesses. Many resources offer programs, classes, and mentorship, but what if a business owner just has a question or needs a little direction on where to go? Which business resource do they call and who do they talk to? It can get pretty confusing or overwhelming at times. Also, many of the resources don't have a diverse staff, which sometimes can create a challenge with connecting with the diverse community. We're hoping this tool will be a solution to all of those challenges and a better resource for our businesses.

Overall, it's been the community that uplifts and supports the Black businesses. The Black Chamber sees itself as the facilitator and navigator for Black businesses and the provider of resources and community support. The chamber has more programs on the horizon, but until then, the Utah business community has the foundation for Black business success.

ASHLEY CLEVELAND

Ashley Cleveland, MCMP, is deputy chief of staff for Salt Lake City Corporation after spending the previous four years planning and running programs for Millcreek City, Utah. In that role, she implemented and coordinated a neighborhood-based effort to close achievement gaps and provide cradle-to-career support for young people and families in Millcreek.

JAMES: *Welcome, Ashley. We're glad to have you here, especially with all the work you've been doing, along with many other Black professionals. I think, with your understanding of city planning, you have a unique perspective on how things are changing.*

ASHLEY: These past five years, I feel like I've met so many amazing Black people that have either been here for a while or have just moved here. They're collaborating and getting stuff done. It's just beautiful to see them moving in their own lane and flourishing based off their interests.

JAMES: *What do you think is helping to make that happen?*

ASHLEY: Well, I think one reason is the mindset. I think a lot of Black people who move here are the type of people who are open to adventure, willing to explore, willing to give things a try and make mistakes. They aren't afraid to give something of themselves, to try something and see whether it will come to fruition. I also think the allies that live here, the people who want to collaborate, are genuinely excited.

JAMES: *For me, being a native, I didn't know what we didn't have. As I got to travel outside the state, I saw what we could look like. It's always great to hear from others that people are finding their way here and we're growing.*

ASHLEY: You know, a lot of us either come here for a job or for education, but when you come here for education, you don't always get to stay. There aren't always jobs in your field. It's a blessing to know that a lot of people that have moved here and got their degree here are now actually working in their field and finding opportunity here. The pipelines are happening, and that's really great, really affirming.

JAMES: *One thing we're seeing is that talent is in such high demand. We are working to be an innovation hub, but that requires more bodies and more skilled talent. We haven't reached our plateau yet. What do you think it will take for that to happen?*

ASHLEY: I think our [state] Office of Economic Development has a really keen eye. I think if we keep building on the momentum we've had for the past five years, I give us another ten to fifteen years to get there. It already looks so different. In just the years I've been here, I've seen a change. When I graduated in 2016, we had, just in Salt Lake City or Salt Lake County, a housing deficit of about seventy-five thousand units. Now, five years later, we have a deficit of about forty thousand. So we've been able to build thirty-five thousand housing units within five years. If we keep that same momentum with jobs and also support everyone moving here, it will look very, very different in the next ten to fifteen years.

> " If we keep that same momentum
> with jobs and also support everyone moving
> here, it will look very, very different in the
> next ten to fifteen years. "

—ASHLEY CLEVELAND

JAMES: *So you've been here seven years and seen this huge transformation. Tell us a little about where you were prior to moving here. What's your journey?*

ASHLEY: Well, I'm a Georgia girl. My dad's side of the family is from Atlanta; my mom's side is from Athens—go, Georgia Bulldogs.

Ashley with daughter hiking

My mom moved us to California when I was very young, so I also consider myself culturally to be a California kid. We did a lot of journeying around the West Coast, Pacific Northwest, but we always came back to California. The longest I ever lived anywhere was Ventura County, or actually Terry County, a small county right above Santa Monica and Santa Barbara. It has a diverse population of migrant workers and a lot of electronics workers, some Filipino, a few Black people. I was one of the few. I lived there from age sixteen to twenty-six. It formed most of my adult life. I came here for grad school. My undergrad is in environmental science. I went to community college as a first-generation college student, then I transferred to Cal State University Channel Islands. One of the things that makes it unique, which I love, is that it's an adaptive reuse campus, meaning an old building turned into a campus. Most buildings have a life of twenty to fifty years, depending on how well they're built, and this used to be a state hospital. They refurbished the whole campus and turned it into dorms, research facilities, labs and a beautiful library that I just adore.

I was the first African American to graduate from their environmental science program. I had a really great mentor, Sean Anderson, who taught me the importance of research and the value of actually getting out from behind your desk and your computer. That's something that stayed with me even when I became a city planner. I spent time learning to be a field biologist, out in the middle of nowhere, trying to be a steward of the environment. That's when I became really interested in ecology, the study of organisms and their relationship to their environment. That's similar to population dynamics. Those are some of the same principles that you use in city planning. At the end of the day, humans are organisms, and our environment is our city.

The whole reason I got my degree in environmental science was because I feel really passionate about environmental justice, right? So after four years of being out in these beautiful landscapes, I was taking my lunch break and thinking all these wonderful large government organizations are purchasing land to conserve it and protect it from all the negative externalities that come out of the city: poor air quality, contamination, congestion, all those things that bring down your quality of life as a human. Instead of running around using all this money to conserve land—which, of course, I don't think is a bad thing—why don't we make the root of the issue better? How do we actually make cities better? How do we make things healthier for humans? That's when I came across human ecology. It led me to city planning. My professor forwarded my CV to the University of Utah to their interim chair, and she was the only one to not respond to my email within a month—but she was actually excited about my prior experience and my background. She was like can you come here? Can you move here now? I was working on the island and was like, "Utah? I don't think so." After initially saying no, I did a little bit more research and found that we have really great access to the outdoors, and that's something that has always brought me a lot of peace.

You know, most of the time people who love the outdoors also love urban fabric. Think of Denver or Portland. Honestly, our infrastructure here, in regards to transportation and proximity to the outdoors, is amazing. You can be from Salt Lake City Airport to the outdoors within forty-five minutes on public transportation. I love Denver, but if you want to go skiing, it's going to be a three-hour drive. Our mountains are really close, and they look like postcards. Everything here is actually close. The outdoors and the opportunities are what led me here.

France, a licensed physician assistant, specializes in psychiatry and behavioral medicine. He's been practicing medicine for more than ten years and built a wide range of experience. He's also part of the inpatient psychiatry staff at Salt Lake Behavioral Health. Melanie, owner of Planted Healing Mental Health Practice, is a speaker, educator, child advocate, and psychotherapist. Together, they have co-founded Continuum Mind Body Collaborative. Melanie is also co-founder of The Black Clinicians practitioner group and a PhD student in The George Washington University's School of Medicine Health Sciences program.

JAMES: *Tell us a little bit about your background and what you're doing now.*

MELANIE: So the last four months, we've been under construction, opening a wellness space. It's called Continuum Mind Body Collaborative. We were in private practice prior. I was in private practice, and France was dipping in a little bit as a medical director, but we realized we wanted to have a more collaborative space where there were more resources for mental health, and we also wanted to incorporate mind and body care. So we finally opened a couple of weeks ago with two other partners, Katie and Amanda. And we have a space now that has five mental health providers. We have yoga, we have body workers, we have functional nutritionists, and psychiatric med management—trying to bring in everything for mental health care.

We had started out with Empath Healing and Wellness and

rebranded to Planted Healing. With this change, moving into this collaborative space, we still have our individual practice. Then in this collaborative space, there are multiple different practices. So everyone who rents space in this building from us has their own private practice.

JAMES: *France is also starting his own mental health services. What is that about?*

FRANCE: I practice psychiatry and medication management focused on adult psychiatry and perinatal psychiatry. So I'm working with pregnant women and women who are looking at pregnancy or breastfeeding, helping them manage medications.

JAMES: *So what has been your journey from your first interest in going into the healthcare industry, and how did it lead you to where you are now?*

FRANCE: I had a plan for a while to go into medicine, and physician's assistant school seemed like the best route for me in terms of timing and cost. Once I got out, I initially was in orthopedic surgery, and I did that for four years: orthopedic spine, mixed with some pediatric orthopedic surgery. I just felt more interested in the psychological aspects of my patients. Melanie was getting her master's at the time, thinking of therapy and psychotherapy. I felt like psychiatry fit me in terms of my passion, and I've been down that route for the last nine years. I dabbled in some private practice initially, and then ended up in hospital psychiatry, and I'm doing that now with the University of Utah. I'll be opening this practice on the side.

MELANIE: The feedback that I hear from my clients that I've sent to him, it's like, "Oh my gosh, he's so talented, I felt like he actually really got me." Or for people who have had difficulty finding the right kind of medications, he's been able to help them find things that work.

FRANCE: Well, I come from a different background—raised in the church. My dad went into nursing homes and hospitals and interacted with people from the church. You gain that type of knowledge and understanding of people, seeing people in a different way, and that's just how I run my practice.

JAMES: *Did Melanie's journey influence you?*

FRANCE: It definitely did, from what she was interested in doing and the way that she practiced to the type of healthcare and medicine that she ended up going into. I think now as we grow, we're building businesses, and I watch her and how hardworking she is and how much time and effort she puts into it, and I see the success that she's had. It pushes me to want to be like that. The way that

France Davis II

she goes about things and the work that she puts in, day in and day out, it's amazing.

JAMES: *Melanie, share with us a little bit about your journey of coming into wellness.*

MELANIE: Someone gave me some really wonderful advice in my early twenties: "Do what you love and be authentic. Don't spend a day doing something that you're not passionate about." And I really took that to heart. I've always kind of attracted older wisdom, and this woman was in her fifties. I really loved that advice. After growing up here, I didn't know what I wanted to do. For undergrad, I thought, *Oh, people are interesting, I'll major in sociology,* but it was kind of just an easy major. But then as I got out into the world and started working and trying different jobs, I felt a real drive and calling to want to work with people and to want to help improve people's lives.

I think it's because it was always something I was always working on. Also, I always wanted to know how I could grow. How can I have better mental health? I think you're your own first subject if you're someone who's a practitioner of any kind. I think you're often thinking about your family and yourself and how to be better. That's where I was inspired to go into mental health in the beginning.

> " I think you're your own first subject if you're someone who's a practitioner of any kind. I think you're often thinking about your family and yourself and how to be better. "

> **—MELANIE DAVIS**

Melanie Davis

At that point, once you have your eyes set on something, especially in our fields, even though they're very different, you kind of just start to build your foundation, right? So, you know, my first job doing clinical work was in a state psychiatric hospital in Kentucky. There were nights I didn't know if I wouldn't come out of there. It was actually kind of scary. There is some element of hazing that happens also, when you're a psych tech. You're new, you can go sit with the rapist or the person who was convicted of murdering their neighbor over a lawn mower. I did my time, building clinical hours. Then when we moved back to Utah, I started to kind of focus my energy more on things that I really enjoyed, but still building clinically and gaining experience, and then school and all of those things.

I think the whole path has really been exploring why people need to live lives that they feel are balanced and that feel authentic and comfortable. Mental health is just a huge part of it. So I've always kind of unfolded that way. When I opened my practice, Empath, Healing and Wellness, now Planted Healing, I think the big thing was that I had been in a space where it felt very centered on the white community in Utah. I did bring in a diverse client population, but again, there's a need here, and it's not being met. How can we meet this for the community? That's when we opened our own practice and felt like this is a space that is safe for the BIPOC community here and everyone's welcome. I have white clients, but this is uniquely a space that needs to be safe at all times for the community of color.

Now CEO of Seonim Consulting, a firm aimed at helping individuals, organizations, companies, and communities succeed, Oz spent twenty-two years in the food and beverage industry, including catering experience in New York City, before he launched Melange Liquid Catering. He's also a directors' board member at Visit Salt Lake and chair of the organization's membership committee. He's raised a family here and has a very driven, connective perspective on how to succeed in business and in life in general.

JAMES: *Let's talk about your journey. You're from Brooklyn, New York, so how did you wind up in Utah?*

OZ: Originally I'm from Jamaica. I've lived in Brooklyn, New York, and New Haven, Connecticut. I spent a year in Okinawa, Japan. I've visited seven or eight countries, spent some time across the East Coast and West Coast. That's from being in the Marine Corps. When I share with people that I'm not supposed to be here, that there's a reason other than myself I'm here, I truly believe that. There are so many instances I could share about why I should not be here, but I truly believe in a higher power, a higher force—call it God or Gaia or whatever you want. So I visited Utah, and I knew it was not one of the fifty states I wanted to live in at that time. I had come to visit a friend, and when I flew back to Queens, I had that inclination, a calling that said, *Move to Utah.* I said, *God, no, no, I'll take any place else.* But within thirty days, I packed up, bought a one-way ticket, and moved to Utah. That happened in 1995. That's the true version of why I'm here—not for college, not for sports, not for a beautiful young lady.

Also, I truly believe I was asked to come here to help create change—or shake it up, depending on who you're talking to—because Utah is a beautiful, beautiful place with beautiful people, but we were lacking in the wholeness or the roundness of the American experience.

JAMES: *Can you expand on that a little bit?*

OZ: So when I first came to Utah and people would discover I was not part of the predominant religion, they would stop engaging me. This was more than twenty years ago now. So how do you deal with that? I chose to teach with humor. I noticed that trend for a while in other places, too. Often you're from Brooklyn and you look brown, people expect you to have ghetto speak. Down South, we were doing a parade, and I was the first person like me that they'd ever seen. But I know I am part of the American experience, and for people to not understand that there are variations—brown, white, yellow, whatever color you want to call us—they are missing something. We are all part of the American experience, and so many people have been insulated from that.

JAMES: *That's great. As you say, Utah has always been underexposed. So this was back twenty-five years ago or so. How has Utah evolved over the last quarter of a century? What did you start diving into when you came here to shake it up?*

OZ: So one of the first things I discovered is, even with a stellar resume—ten years in the Marine Corps and experience as an entrepreneur in Brooklyn—people will disregard you because of the color of your skin. So I needed a job. My father had taught me that if you know how to set a table, you can find work in this world. So I entered the world of hospitality, but no one was looking to hire someone like me. That's also where, I think, the blessings lie. I started to work for some amazing people eventually, including a lot of public figures. I have served every sitting governor. I was privileged to be invited to homes and offices on the hills, where it might be this handful of dignitaries and myself. I'm privileged to be part of that very narrow group who was respected and passed muster, so to speak, to be included with some of the power brokers.

JAMES: *So how did you get in the door?*

OZ: I think it has to do with the integrity factor. I do not post on Instagram or Facebook or have an email newsletter. When you actually look into another person's eyes and smile and say, "Thank you. How are you?" Or you say, "Let me get something for you," and you make something special that is crafted for that person, that matters. I think the gift is to be able to understand or identify certain needs of my clients. In most cases, it's not about a fancy drink. It's about how you energetically, spiritually, and intentionally serve someone in that moment.

JAMES: *So you elevate those connections. It's deeper than serving a drink. That's wonderful. Let's talk a little about your family. Your daughter and son are following in your footsteps with military careers?*

OZ: Right now, my daughter is in a Navy Academy, and my son is returning home from training with the Army National Guard, yes.

JAMES: *As a parent and as the kind of entrepreneur you've proven yourself to be, I'm sure you have a unique perspective. What advice would you give to young people or Black businesses?*

OZ: Okay, this is going to sound odd, but I'm going to ask every Black business owner to stop viewing themselves as a Black business owner. You are a beautiful, dynamic American. First of all, the cottage industry is what made America successful. From the beginning, it was the mom and pop small business, it was a midsize entrepreneur. So the first thing I would like to say is, *Stop viewing yourself as a Black business owner*—unless there's a grant that says *Black business owner*. But for me, I found that when you label yourself something, you let the connotations change your experience. When I came to Utah and became a business owner, I thought about whether I should identify myself as a Black business owner back in 1998. Why would I do that? What would be the benefit of that? Coming from Brooklyn, we had no *Black business owners* because there were Black business owners everywhere. I was not raised with this mindset of calling myself that. Call yourself an American institution and an American necessity, because when my family had an entrepreneurial endeavor, we were the only ones hiring kids from fourteen to eighteen years old, and that was a time and place where their only other option was to sell drugs on the corner. When you have that positivity, you will develop a forward-thinking frame of mind, and then you'll realize you're creating opportunities for your family, for your community, for your county, your city or state, and ultimately, your country and the globe. Focus on being the best you. There are so many people that want to see you succeed. Instead of focusing on our task and our problems, we need to connect with a wider audience.

" When you have that positivity, you will develop a forward-thinking frame of mind, and then you'll realize you're creating opportunities for your family, for your community, for your county, your city or state, and ultimately, your country and the globe. "

—OZ HUTTON

Working in debt collection for decades now, Steven Johnson takes a unique approach to his calling. He sees the need for financial literacy and uplifting others. Now his business, launched when he returned to Utah after expanding into commercial accounts in Ohio, brings a uniquely experienced blend of expertise to help both clients and those who have fallen into debt.

JAMES: *Steve, thanks for sharing your perspective. Let's start out with your business. If I were to tell someone what Luke, Johnson & Lewis is, what is my thirty-second pitch?*

STEVEN JOHNSON: Luke, Johnson & Lewis is a collection agency with a three-tier component. We do strategic consulting. We do, obviously, debt collection. And then we do a third component, which is auto repossession. I've been in the financial industry for over thirty years. My partner's been in the industry for over twenty years. And I mean, I've held every position, from collection agent to repo agent to consultant.

So we've got a lot of experience in what we offer. We really break it down with strategic consulting and offer a designated and foolproof plan that helps your business resolve delinquent accounts. If you are a company who struggles with slow payments or account management, we can come in and do a consultation, and your first consultation is free. We can come in and give you a process for reacting with a quicker time, a strategy you can put into place with literature or a call strategy. We can basically show you how to move and shift your receivables and put them in positions where they don't go into delinquency. As far as our debt collection, we have a dedicated team with account managers who oversee the results of your accounts. We're dedicated to productively closing delinquent accounts in a timely manner. I mean, a lot of people, their mistake is they let stuff go out too far.

This is the exciting part, for me. A lot of people make the mistake of allowing their accounts to go out too far without communication, without interaction. So we have a formula where we take care of that in a two-step process. A lot of people perceive collections to be a gritty game when, you know, any time they've had interaction with a collection agent, or a collection agency, or something of that nature, it's always been abrasive. What we develop is a more humane approach to dealing with people that allows them to have some dignity. We can help to get them back into financial stability.

With our other tier, auto possession, we've had great results. We had companies hire us to do anything from a motorcycle to a truck, car, or boat. We have award-winning recovery tools. There's nothing we can't do.

JAMES: *I like the emphasis on a humane approach. As you mentioned, you've built some serious experience.*

STEVEN: Back when I fell into this, a long, long time ago, the tech really didn't exist. We got our information on flashcards from the library. The public library was the biggest source of information to conduct your investigation. So you know what, I think it was my first year of college, and I was looking for something I could do on my own time. I had seen an ad that they had in the paper for collection agents.

I became great at it because I produced dialogue that his team wasn't using. I got people to feel comfortable talking with me and making commitments to me as well. I ran with it and became the best person on the floor. And then I became a team leader, and then a project manager and topped out. I just liked the game. I liked the industry. And, you know, I like helping people with information that they never knew existed, and a lot of people still don't know how to improve your credit score or how to pay off accounts sooner and eliminate some of that interest. There's a lot of information and finances that people don't know, and I like to teach.

JAMES: *I want to rewind real quick, because you did two stints in Utah, and your second stint was 2008/2009. What brought you to Utah the first time, and when was that?*

STEVEN: My ex-wife brought me to Utah, in 2002. Her sister lived here and was going through a divorce. Our mission was to come out here to help her in that transition. So we came out here and helped our sister go through her transition, and then, you know, that whole thing kind of put a wedge between me and her, we grew into different people. So we agreed to separate and terminate that marriage.

So I adapt. I was a free agent. I did that for a while, and then I met a really wonderful lady. She was originally from Scotland, grew up in England, and we just meshed immediately. Long story short, we got married, and immediately, she's recruited for a position in Cleveland, Ohio. At the time, I was working for a law firm here called Riddle & Associates. I was on the fast track of, you know, being the top person there, but I realize I'm going to have to take a backseat. That was her dream, because the job that they were offering her at Cleveland was what she wanted to do, what she was built for. That's besides the fact that they were going to pay her three or four times more than I was making.

We decide: Let's do it. I told Riddle what I was planning, and he asked me to stay on for three months. I had just started the beta site in a place called Ephraim, Utah. My job was to go and set up the infrastructure as far as choosing the location, getting the tech inserted, doing the job fair, hiring all the personnel and getting that thing up and going.

By the time I left there, that beta site office was basically out-collecting our home base. At that point, he really didn't want me to leave, and offered me more money to stay, but I couldn't. I made a commitment to my wife. I went out to Ohio full time. The people were different. The place was strange. The only thing that was cool is they had just gotten Lebron James. The company that my wife was working for at the time had a box there.

I did find work doing something similar to what I had been doing, a law firm called McCarthy, Burgess & Wolff. I'd met with Steve Wolff and he was so cool. He was ultra-aggressive in the business world. I mean, he had a whole different format and a plan for acceleration with the collection process. And he had major clients. He put me in the leasing department. This was my first time collecting commercial. I had done consumer forever. I'd done some repossession, but I'd never done commercial, and it was on a different scale. The difference between consumer and commercial is a lot more money. In consumer, you're dealing with people who may owe you $10,000 or $20,000. But in the commercial world, you're dealing with businesses that may owe you half a million or a million. I learned different tricks and was able to add more tools to my bag doing their commercial. It opened up a whole other world for me.

I celebrated that, and I was good at it. Things were going great, but it was a change. I kind of missed Utah, because I still had ties here. Some of the firms I work for were still trying to get me back. Things were changing in that relationship, too. We parted ways, and I came back out here to Utah. I can't remember the reason but I met with my partner, Preston. I was telling him the emotional and mental state that I was in, and he was like, "Man, you should just come back here." I met with the GM at Gillette and Paul Law Offices, and he offered me something I couldn't turn down.

JAMES: *What was it about Utah that you were missing?*

STEVEN: People. Camaraderie. Utah is a great place for building relationships. Great for raising your kids. It was clean, untouched. You know, it was like a hidden gem. When I first came to Utah, you could still just go to the gas pump and just start pumping gas and everybody spoke to you. It was a different utopia for me. Another thing here was the scenery. You could live in Salt Lake and you could see the mountains and feel like you were in a wonderland.

" Utah is a great place for building relationships. Great for raising your kids. "

—STEVEN JOHNSON

JAMES: *So when it comes to being a small business and being a Black small business owner, what was that like for you?*

STEVEN: It was rough. But you know what, I really have to credit you and the Utah Black Chamber for helping me. The tools that are needed, the access, the chamber put me in a lot of great positions to learn how to grow, to operate a business, to maintain a business.

At the same time, there was learning as you grow. You've got to be fearless as a business owner. There are a lot of doors that you just have to keep knocking on before they open. My challenge was finding tools. I can really say that I benefited from a lot of the stuff that the chamber brought, because there were a lot of people who I met who helped me understand what I needed to do, where I needed to be, how aggressive to be, when to be aggressive, how to time-manage.

You were really good at helping me with time management. Other people who were brought onto our team at the chamber really, really embraced me and helped me. I took that and recorded and archived it. Every time I see something or hear something more, I save it to bring it back from the archive and use at a later date.

I remember one time you came, and I was having problems getting a line of credit. You came out and you met me at the bank president's house. Before you left, you said: "I'm not going to let you fail. I'm not ever going to give up on you." That stuck with me. I replay that all the time when I'm trying to help somebody or do something now. I want to make them feel how you made me feel. *I'm gonna keep trying to pick you up. I'm gonna keep trying to push you.*

MARCUS JONES

Marcus Jones is a native of Phoenix, Arizona, who played college football at University of Utah, and has since made a name for himself as the proprietor of Miss Essie's Southern BBQ. He's been the company president for eighteen years and counting, offering smoked meats and barbecue sauce and catering to a community always hungry for more.

JAMES: *So tell us how you went from college football to being a small business owner?*

MARCUS: I was really hoping to make the pros. Then I realized I had my family and a daughter. So life became real. I had bills and my daughter was crying one day, and I realized I had to be the daddy and be the provider. I wasn't really ready for that. At the time I was immature, like every young man, going through those phases and maturity. As I got older, I had to really figure out what I wanted to do.

As far as a career, I knew I hated the 9-to-5, hated people telling me what to do. I just didn't see any purpose for me to be working for somebody if I just wasn't happy, you know? I had to come to a real-life realization, teach myself a lot of stuff in business. I had to learn some articulation, if you will: how to talk, how to write contracts, how to read a contract, understand cash, understand money in and money out, staying out of debt, what's assets, what's not assets—all of that.

Miss Essie's kind of fell in my lap. I worked on my dad, brought him out here and just really grew the business from there. He was the back-end guy who's in the kitchen, and he didn't want to be put in the spotlight. I was the guy who kind of multitasked. I was in the back, with some of the recipes he knew, trying to replicate them. I was younger, and I felt more comfortable being in front of the camera, talking—because they teach us stuff in college sports like how to talk when you're under pressure, when your emotions are all jacked up and you're upset.

That part came pretty easy to me. Then I had to start thinking about how my dad is getting older and how we have to start making transitions where we needed to really mitigate that risk of what would happen if something should happen to him, or to me, going forward. So we got together with a company called SkyBox Sports Grill. That was our first big foray. All we knew before that was how to cook the food, essentially. When you've got cooks like my dad or you know, your grandma, they don't really have a recipe. They just know it. Going into business and trying to scale up recipes, trying to be more consistent across the board, we had to grow. You need to have some kind of recipe in place to make sure you're not wasting money.

JAMES: *One thing that I picked up there about transitioning into the business world is what you were talking about how football applied to your business acumen, like knowing how to talk in front of people.*

MARCUS: Not only that, but also just the fact of waking up early in the morning to hustle. It takes really applying yourself in things that maybe you're just not too comfortable with and being willing to fail, knowing you're going to get better as time goes on. That's the mentality.

" It takes really applying yourself in things that maybe you're just not too comfortable with and being willing to fail, knowing you're going to get better as time goes on. "

—MARCUS JONES

JAMES: *Why did you choose something you didn't know how to do?*

MARCUS: Honestly, my dad approached me with it. I had worked once at SkyBox, and it was apparent to me what I wanted to be. I just saw an opportunity to really fill in somewhere where I fit. I saw an opportunity to go places where I've never been before. You see the employee life, and then you see what it's like to be an entrepreneur. That life opens you up to a whole new world of people, a whole new world of money, a whole new world of resources. All that, as an employee, you just never would have.

I had been a waiter, but also it's the same if you're working with data entry or something like that; there's only so much that you get exposed to. I just loved the idea of getting exposed to growth and what the possibility of that growth would be— whether it be selling a million dollars of a product or growing our brand nationally or regionally, or just even locally, where everybody knows you. Also, going into food, I knew I would have to teach myself. I loved that idea, and of course, I wanted an opportunity to take care of myself and my family. That didn't happen in football.

JAMES: *So you brought your dad here, though. You wanted to stay here. Why?*

MARCUS: I had my daughter here, and I liked Utah. I really, really liked Utah. I was independent. People knew me. I had a really good church family and a really good structure. I had support. I think moving back to Arizona at that point in time wouldn't have offered the opportunities that I had here. Everybody knew me here, people who are big USU fans that wanted to help out a football player or an athlete, show them some love. If I didn't play football, I would have missed the doors that opened up for me, if that makes sense.

Since then, I've had the chance to see Utah grow, the state and the city. When I first got here, I hated it: one-lane roads and country music. Arizona was a bit more diversified. It's been eye-opening in the way that I got to see Utah really grow, bringing in new tech companies, new restaurants, new cultures to make this a beautiful state to live in.

JAMES: *Last question: Who is Miss Essie?*

MARCUS: Miss Essie May Jones is my grandmother. She was the anchor on my dad's side of the family and raised eight kids. She held down a full-time job, and she took care of the sick. I don't know how she did it. She will take people in and, just as they are ending their life, she will be that caretaker for the family. When I cook any kind of food or barbecue sauce, that pushes me because she was bogged down. She had babies; she had eight kids. She held down the fort and was a very religious, spiritual person. With the heart that she had, she was able to do a lot more than other people could. She overextended herself, but the gifts were the feedback she got. For me, my way of caretaking is bringing food to the community. If I'm having a hard day, all I do is remember what my grandmother did. I have to pull from that, from where I came from, to give me perspective and a goal for where I want to go. It helps energize me and give me that little bit of push.

Marlon Lindsay is the founder and CEO of 21stCenEd and cofounder and CEO of TechTrep. His work helps to ensure that children of color have access to solid STEM educational opportunities, no matter where they live. A native of Jamaica, he moved to the United States to seek opportunity. His work to help school districts assist homeschooling families led to discovering a great need in the educational sphere and in the community at large.

JAMES: *Marlon, welcome. Tell us about 21stCenEd and how that evolved.*

MARLON: TechTrep Academy is a virtual school that partners with school districts to provide comprehensive education to homeschoolers. We are focusing on technology and entrepreneurship as a way to prepare our students for the rest of the twenty-first century. That was our model, and we spun off to address the public school market.

It's been a calling. You start a company to secure the financial future of your family and to do some good work. Then you get into it, and you become intimate with the marketplace, and you really understand the issues. You shift from trying to make a dollar to trying to make a difference. At some point in every entrepreneur's life, you shift your focus from financial security to really making a difference, and it becomes a calling. That happened for me about two-and-a-half years in. I traveled across the country to look at what was being done in public education and then talked to a whole lot of folks—superintendents, teachers, students. We realized that we were at a point where we need to think about education differently. It's an ocean liner, in terms of the change we need, versus a speedboat. It really does have to change with the advancement of our technologies. That's why we have to get the work done.

JAMES: *And how long have you been working on it now?*

MARLON: For going on five years, we've been in the middle of changing from TechTrep to 21stCenEd. The work we've evolved into has become much bigger than just providing STEM education. Our core purpose is to provide STEM education for all students. That has to happen early, often, and everywhere. That's our value proposition. But to do that, you really have to organize the community around them so they can identify the skills and talents they need for the local community and region in terms of workforce development. Then you have to establish these community partnerships so you can create a network, almost an ecosystem, where not only are the students accessing STEM education in school, after school, and out of school, but they also have strong, ubiquitous access within the community. And it has to be for all students. That's how we transform and sustain: Get the entire community involved. That means we do curriculum development, plus community organizing, plus culture shifting.

JAMES: *Talk to me about the focus on twenty-first century skills. Is that not already happening?*

MARLON: Think about how many jobs already have been eliminated and will be eliminated. My first job was at McDonald's. If you've walked into a McDonald's lately, you'll know there's a kiosk where you order. Then some have a burger-making machine, robots making fries. A lot of the jobs that we used to do are now being automated. So for your high school student, what kind of first job are they going to get? Well, it's maintaining those robots, reprogramming them, etc. So we have to make sure our students are prepared for that. Context is everything, too. It's cool to have it in schools—and we must—but the community also has to be aware that there's transformation going on around them. It's that story about a frog in hot water. You don't know that it's boiling until it's too late. I feel like sometimes, in many communities, we're sitting in hot water. It's getting hotter and hotter. We need to take action before it's too late. So part of my work is to make sure that we tie all the pieces together so we can transform as a community and as a society.

> " Part of my work is to make sure that we tie all the pieces together so we can transform as a community and as a society. "

—MARLON LINDSAY

Byron has enjoyed a storied education and career. A native of the DC area, he was shaped by his experiences with culture: museums as a child and then traveling abroad as a college student and a young man. He's brought a unique perspective to Utah's arts and cultural scenes and his gift for building connections has set the stage for a successful consulting venture, Byron Russell LLC, a team of brand consultants, researchers, strategists, and more.

JAMES: *Welcome. I know you've had a lot of worldly experiences and have helped shape some of the cultural opportunities here in Utah, but first, tell us about Byron Russell Consulting.*

BYRON: Well, I've been here in Utah since 1992. I've been doing consulting for ten years. It really started after my experience with the Utah Symphony, and then I moved into banking as a loan executive for a short period at Zions Bank. Then I ended up working Western Governors University. As I kept following that path, I noticed that I was serving the needs of an institution or a business. I thought, *What value would I have if I transfer that to my ability to serve clients?* I could utilize the network that allowed me to work at a bank or at the university or the symphony. What if I applied that to a business model that allowed my network to help support the needs of these companies and businesses?

So that became Byron Russell LLC. My friend and yours, Scott Anderson, was a mentor of mine who advised me that my name has a brand and I needed to utilize that brand. Then, as I began to bring clients on with that model for value, I began to get in the big league of a lot of large, multinational companies that were looking for various skills. So I expanded my business to three partners. There were four of us altogether. Lizzie Barlow in Reno, Ronnie Peters in New York City, and Monte Caldwell and me here in Salt Lake City. The four of us bring different skills. We go to a client armed not only with my network, which is very helpful, but also with the skills that we have to meet the needs of growing, successful companies. There are ones that aren't growing and are struggling to have a budget to pay me, but they have growing pains, they have unique issues, and they have various strengths. To help them with those established goals, we start with discovery. My tagline is, *ideas, connections, results.* We work with a company through a discovery, sit down and work through learning more about them, their needs, and our talents. Then there's a design process, after which we deploy the actionable opportunities to advance their brand or their value. That works. A lot of my clients are on a retainer basis, and then sometimes it's a finite window.

JAMES: *So tell me about your journey, then, because you talked about other places you've worked in Utah, and I know you have a great story. Let's start with how you ended up in Salt Lake City.*

BYRON: Well, until about five years old, I was in Washington, DC and South East Anacostia. As anybody who is familiar with DC knows, Anacostia is not exactly the place where one wants to go and live or to be raised.

Fortunately for my family, we were able to move to Maryland, which is right across the border. I lived in Prince George's County, which is also probably not the wealthiest of counties in the Washington, DC area. In fact, it was a very lower middle class, blue-collar community. I was really fortunate to have experienced

Byron Russell

that, because that's why I can sit here and tell you how much I value being here.

I was raised in the Washington, DC area, went to a Catholic school for a while, and then ended up in a public school system. I had some great opportunities and tremendous mentors and education, and I ended up going to the University of Maryland College Park, with a few little interruptions, and they were pretty good interruptions. One was exploratory travel through Europe and down into Egypt. Going to Egypt opened my eyes to the world, to how people live. I had never seen anything like it.

I realized, gosh, the world's a big place, and it's got a lot of variety. And people find a way to live their life. I wanted to learn more. My curiosity drove me to travel the world, and one of my next trips was to South Africa. During apartheid, I went to South Africa to plan an International Youth Conference to bring students from around the world to see what Africa was like with their own eyes, with their own ability to explore and to ask questions and to learn. It was one of the most amazing experiences ever. First of all, South Africa, sadly, because of the apartheid, was also this dichotomy of seeing this beautiful, beautiful place and its rich culture and amazing people—and yet the suffering was very palpable.

So I spent a lot of time working on those issues in my life, and I actually subsequently studied international relations at the University of Maryland. Then I was hired during my travels by a Member of Parliament from Great Britain, David Atkinson from Bournemouth East. He was slated to be one of the Members of Parliament speaking at this conference at Cape Town University. We were both on the agenda to speak there, and then he offered me a job.

So I had another interruption, went to London and worked in the House of Commons. It's probably the greatest experience in my life. It made me understand and realize how important the issues that he focused on were: human rights through his belief in Christian rights, because he was Catholic. As you know, in Great Britain, the majority of churches are Protestant. So what was it like to be a minority and at a place where you were actually a Member of Parliament? I got engaged, and that prospect brought another one of my greatest opportunities, to go to Southwest Africa, which is now in Namibia. And my role was to work to build an independent platform for the transitional government of Southwest Africa, the last colony, which is now in Namibia.

Having that experience just made me realize that my own country can use a little help too, so I came back and got really engaged in just understanding a little bit more about my own country. Constitutional Law was something that I studied and I ended up in DC for work, first at The Washington Post as a journalist in the style section. It was really an entry into journalism. Then I ended up working at The Washington Times, covering the White House and Congress. That, in itself, was an incredible education. It was almost like a constant class.

I looked at journalism as a continuation of learning. You do almost have a midterm every week, which is called the deadline. And it was really fascinating, exhilarating, and exhausting. At some point, I realized I needed to find something that I was really passionate about. I saw a longer runway.

I just took a break and found some desert, which reminded me of Namibia, and traveled to White Sands, New Mexico, of all places, inspired by an Ansel Adams portrait. As I drove up to Utah and saw these amazing mountains in the spring covered with beautiful white snow over electric green. I just thought it was going to be fun.

So, I decided to move here, and that was in 1992. I found myself in a place that had natural beauty and had incredible quality of life. There were some areas that I found lacking. Instead of complaining about them, I decided to do something about it. In particular was the arts. Having had a chance to be on the East Coast and enjoy New York and DC and the arts scenes there, and also then in London, which has the greatest theatre, musicals, and the most amazing visual arts, I saw that lacking here in Utah. I had an opportunity to actually work on the very first ZAP campaign—the Zoo, Arts & Parks campaign. By conduit, I worked at the Utah Symphony, in development. And that was really exciting because I was working with a team and leading a campaign to make sure that the arts could be vibrant, that they could expand, and they could offer some of the joy that I experienced.

I fell in love with the idea that the arts could be sustained.

That was really me following my passion, and that passion is what created the network that I still have today. *If you follow your passion, your passion will build for you what you need to construct in life.* I now have a network of people who like doing what I do. I may not be able to go to my private jet and have a bite someplace, but I can go to the symphony with them, I can be on boards with them. My passion lends me to be in that place. I think when you find those passions, you shouldn't shy away from them because they feel good or are fun. Isn't that what life should be? You gravitate towards things in life that are good. Greek philosophy, as flawed as it is, does teach us how to be better people. Part of that is the experience of our meaning. In Greek, you know, the dramas were a great way for us to learn good and evil, so to speak. And this idea of myth keeps repeating itself. My point is, that's my passion.

" I fell in love with the idea that the arts could be sustained. That was really me following my passion, and that passion is what created the network that I still have today. *If you follow your passion, your passion will build for you what you need to construct in life.* "

—BYRON RUSSELL

FIVE

Emerging Leaders

Martin Luther King, Jr., John Lewis, Sojourner Truth, Ida B. Wells, Malcolm X, and Muhammad Ali. We remember these individuals as Civil Rights leaders, but what we don't think about is that when they were in their prime as activists, they were under the age of forty. Young, determined and resilient, they leveraged their young energy and ambition to be change agents for our country. Martin Luther King, Jr. met with President John F. Kennedy at just thirty-four years old.

When you think about people who brought change to the Black community or any community, history points to individuals in their twenties and thirties. I once heard, "Ignorance on fire is better than knowledge on ice." I feel the older you get, the more resistant you become to change, even when change is for the better. The effort may seem overwhelming or even impossible, but not to these emerging leaders. They haven't had enough "brainwashing of adulting."

In all seriousness, it's the young leaders who have the acute sense of justice when it comes to society issues. With fresh adult eyes, they see problems and are eager to get involved in finding a solution and bring creativity and a new perspective. To others, their approach may not always seem practical, but they uncover hidden assumptions and opportunities that illuminate new pathways forward. Take the evolution of diversity, equity, and inclusion, for example. Within the last two years, we have seen an intense focus on creating a more inclusive environment in the world around us that has led to more conversation, new terminology, and a growth in understanding for all of us, and this has all been led by our emerging young professionals. They lead the trends in our society today, culture, clothes, music, and entertainment. These individuals lead our future and our present.

The growth of Black Utah over the last few years has come from the leadership of our millennials and Gen Z population. Not until recently has Utah had a strong young Black professional population. After graduating high school, many of my friends left Utah to places like Atlanta or other cities to attend a historically Black college and university (HBCU). It was hard and still is challenging today to retain young Black talent. The rapidly increasing population has brought more young Black professionals with ambition and a voice. We see them in various sectors from finance to engineering to healthcare. In the past, you could go weeks before seeing a Black person walking down the street, but today, in downtown Salt Lake City, it is becoming more and more common. What is bringing them here? What are they doing? Most importantly, what is attracting them and wanting them to stay?

Our Black emerging leaders became even more visible within the last couple of years during the peak of the Black Lives Matter movement. We saw them leading protests and events, and we saw an increasing amount of Black businesses and organizations. What is more encouraging and more comforting is that their voice is growing stronger and louder, making it easier for the influencers who have been carrying the torch for so long pass it on to them.

I was thrilled to learn from the contributors to this chapter what inspires them and what they are doing to grow Black Utah. Our creativity and talent in the community has grown significantly. Could Utah catch up with the rest of the popular cities in the country with our new and thriving professionals? Will they be the next generation to add significant growth to the Black population?

AANJEL CLAYTON

Diversity consultant Aanjel Clayton is the Director at New Pattern Utah, a coalition of business leaders supporting Black women founders, and the global DEI strategist and trainer at PowerToFly, which aims to accelerate economic equality by supporting and connecting underrepresented talent to highly visible sectors.

JAMES: *So you grew up north of Salt Lake, but you were raised up in Calvary Baptist Church in Salt Lake City?*

AANJEL: Yeah. My mom's white, my dad's Black, and it was really important for them that my brother and I grew up with some sense of the Black community. My dad's family isn't really around here, so they made a conscious effort. They went to a bunch of different churches in the valley and met Pastor Davis, and then they were like, This is where we're going to raise our kids. I feel like there's a lot of life experiences I learned there that really transitioned well to the work that I do now. I saw my parents lead a youth ministry. I saw them lead a meeting and work with different churches, all kinds of community stuff. I learned a lot of the skills that I use now, today, through Calvary.

JAMES: *I'm curious though. There are a lot of Black Baptist churches in Davis and Weaver counties, so what made them shift to Salt Lake?*

AANJEL: I think for them it was the pastor. Anyone that knows him, knows his family, his style, and how he relates to folks really appreciates him. Just the way that he would tell stories, he was like a world-renowned storyteller. I think as we grew up, we definitely left the nest a little bit and tried out some different stuff. I think like now Christianity is not so church-based. You can stream things online. We've gone to a couple different churches, but I think the community, and Pastor Davis, is really what made them choose Calvary.

JAMES: *So you're doing a lot of work in diversity. What is your sense of how companies are working to become more diverse? How do we increase access? I'm also interested in your take on what we used to call "code switching," where we go into work and because we're Black, we have to act a certain way.*

AANJEL: Being a mixed kid, I never knew that was a thing when I was a child. When I was with my white family, when I was in school with my friends, I just thought that's what everyone else did. So I talked to my dad, and he was like, "Yeah, when I go to work, this is how I have to present myself so people can take me seriously because they come with their own stereotypes and biases." He really broke it down for me. What's really interesting about that, though, is that a lot of companies now, in a post–Civil Rights world and after 2020 with George Floyd and Breonna Taylor, are competing for Black talent in a way that they hadn't before. I think we, as a Black talent network, have said, "Okay, if you want me to work here, this is what I need it to look like." I need to be able to show up authentically and without repercussions. I don't need X, Y, or Z; I'm going to be myself authentically. Companies have had to accept that now. I think there's a lot of pushback from us where we've really leveraged the opportunity and the influence that we've had in this time. Companies are now building spaces where Black people don't have to code switch, where I can have my activism and I don't have to shut it off or turn it off.

I feel like social media has helped increase access to networking, in a really broad way. I'm not an extrovert; people that know me know I would rather be at home. I mean, if I'm an event, I can be, but I don't really like running around the room. Social media networking made it easier for me to be able to reach out to someone on LinkedIn, or on Instagram, or where my networking company does work and I'm on my couch on my phone. So I'm making those connections where I don't have to be that outgoing person, in person.

It's really changed how we interact. For example, I just picked up golf like a couple months ago, and it's such a club. Ultimately, you have to be invited. It's almost like social media and social networking has influenced business, really broadened access. If you think of the way golf clubs used to be, that's where wealthy people would strike deals. We weren't always there. And so now we've really brought the access to everyone through social media networking.

I can DM someone on my personal Instagram, and then they're looking at my personal feed. Your brand has now become accessible. I go to work, and I turn it on all the time. I had to learn very early that you can't have a work persona and a personal persona and an activism persona; they're all the same person. You have to be authentic in all these spaces.

JAMES: *I love that perspective. So tell us a little about your work in DEI and how you're helping to change the landscape here in Utah. We have a lot of people coming in now who fit into the younger age* *group. What types of things do you do that help ensure that Black talent is welcome here and can grow here?*

AANJEL: My DEI journey really started with the Utah focus, with the companies that I was in. It was a lot about a term I use, "the inclusion house." A company really wants to be able to say, "Okay, we've got this house, this organization, and let's get Black talent in here, and we're all for it, right?" And you're like, "I love the enthusiasm; however, you have a back door." And if they're not comfortable, and they feel like they can really sit down in your house, they're going to leave out the back door. They're going to notice some dust bunnies of racism and discrimination and oppression; they'll be like, This place is not really for me. In DEI, I'm all about cleaning up the house before we bring folks in. It's going through the policies. It's going through the procedures to make sure we're building an organization that's inclusive, so when we do make that full switch, we can open up the floodgates.

JAMES: *What are some examples of policies and procedures that should be reviewed?*

AANJEL: When it comes down to retention, it's down to what's happening in their HR world, so that's where I really got my technical training, my degree. There's a lot of room for improvement. I believe it's around three out of ten white HR generalists who cannot identify racism within their own company; however, five out of ten Black HR professionals would say their organization has racism. When someone is experiencing discrimination, they go to HR to think that HR is going to be able to identify, investigate, and rectify a wrong, but they don't have those tools.

I actually experienced that. What got me into this world was I worked in an organization, the N word was said at work in front of my face, and I was just kind of shocked. I never thought I would see that, especially Utah. I went to my HR partner, and they were like, "Okay, the first thing that you need to do is to make sure that you don't retaliate." I had to sign that paper that said, I wouldn't retaliate against the person that had said that. When we talk about HR and the tools and like what we are taught as HR practitioners, we're not taught how to facilitate racial issues within an organization or racial conflict. That's one thing that I think organizations can really start to focus on: giving their HR programs the tools to be able to handle these situations and to be able to not be uncomfortable. I felt like, as a Black employee, I was leading the conversation. I was educating while I was dealing with my own trauma.

It definitely created an anger in me. That's just how I am. I wish I could be the person that's quiet, but I just don't work that way. That's really when I was looking at where I wanted to go with my career. That experience changed the trajectory of where I wanted to be.

JAMES: *How did you get there?*

AANJEL: So I studied business administration with an HR management emphasis, and then I got a change management and business certification. When I got my certification through Cornell, it was my degree coupled with a couple different certifications that I've got throughout my different jobs. I really built this technical side, but then you also need the experience, right? A lot of times I was trying to pitch myself to these different organizations, they're like, "Look, the technical side is great, but you don't have the experience." So I was like, "All right, well, I can wait another ten years to hopefully get into a job and build up enough experience to then get to the level that I want, or I can take on a second job working fairly crazy hours outside of my schedule, just to gather experience." I had a friend that I met who was a head of DEI at Zions, and I worked with her on Zions DEI. Then she left Zions and opened up her own practice, and I worked with her outside of my like 9 to 5 and gathered that experience. So that's really where I got my first break. Someone took a chance on me. Now these other organizations have seen me and my drive and passion, and then another woman of color invited me to come on over. That really sparked everything.

JAMES: *I love that. And I think that speaks to what you were saying earlier, about the doors opening. How do we open up more doors?*

AANJEL: I use the term "doorstopper." It's like, I might get into a room at my job. I might be the only woman at this table, or I might be the only person of color at the table, so I need to put a doorstopper in that door and make sure it stays open. I need to bring my people in with me, right? You don't get a medal for being the only one. I'm not any better because I'm the only one in this room, and also we don't get a rich diversity of perspective if I'm speaking for all Black people of color or for all women. Because my unique experience is so different from even yours, or someone else in Utah. It's so varied. I think companies want to amplify voices; however, they want to amplify one voice, and sometimes that one voice is so unique that they don't give that broad perspective. I really love that in Utah, women of color, specifically Black women, really make an effort. It's not cute to be the only Black woman at the table anymore. We need to bring other perspectives with us.

" I might be the only woman at this table, or I might be the only person of color at the table, so I need to put a doorstopper in that door and make sure it stays open. I need to bring my people in with me, right? You don't get a medal for being the only one. I'm not any better because I'm the only one in this room, and also we don't get a rich diversity of perspective if I'm speaking for all Black people of color or for all women. "

—AANJEL CLAYTON

ALYSSHA (DAIRSOW) AND
MELIGHA GARFIELD

Alyssha is a New Jersey native who moved to Salt Lake City about eight years ago. She's also the founder of Curly Me!, focused on supporting young Black girls, ages five to fourteen. The organization provides mentoring and hosts events to help children of color embrace their best selves.

Meligha grew up in Rochester, New York, and moved to the area in 2019 to serve as the inaugural director of the Black Cultural Center at University of Utah.

This young married couple met at a Juneteenth event, and their romance blossomed as Alyssha offered to show the newcomer around downtown Salt Lake City. Meligha's intentional approach to pursuing a relationship and Alyssha's outgoing nature, which led her to offer to be the unofficial tour guide for downtown, make for a balanced match.

JAMES: *It's a small Black community here, and it takes a village to raise a village. You two are part of the next in line to pioneer this path here in Utah. Let's start with you, Alyssha. Tell us a little about your journey.*

ALYSSHA: I touched down in 2013. I did not plan on being here this long—honest to God, two years, max. By my third year, I was in a graduate program. After the first year, you're still on your journey of figuring out what life is. And so two years pass, then a third year comes up, and Curly Me! goes from an idea to a bigger idea. And then 2016 comes and more events happen, and 2017 comes

123

and you're really starting to get out there, and in 2018, we became a nonprofit. So that was like a we're *here here* moment.

I had moved from a fast-paced, very involved area. Back home in New Jersey, there was always something to get involved in. You're still a minority, but there are so many cultures and so many places where you can go in a short amount of time. When I moved to Utah, I was just like, *This is slow. This is beautiful.* I wanted to enjoy it, but I would still picture myself, in the future, talking about that time in my life that I lived in Utah.

But when I realized that I was going to be staying here a lot longer, I was like, *How am I going to make my presence here? What am I going to find to do outside of my comfort zone? How am I going to make friends with people that I may not have the same background as, whether that's faith-wise, or just community involvement? How can I get to know more people, because I'm an extrovert.*

I've learned a lot about myself and what I need to do to thrive in a place like Utah. You start to really realize your family is not close. You have to do things for you. For me, it's a lot of just being in the Utah streets, going to various places, whether that's an opportunity to go skydiving, see the Colorado River, or find live music. Had I been in New Jersey, I don't know if I would have put myself out there like that. It was me and my journey. I started to make my own decisions, started to become my own person, started to be who Alyssha was supposed to be.

JAMES: *You're just spreading your wings, experiencing all new things, new landscapes.*

ALYSSHA: The mountains never cease to amaze me. It's like they change, but they don't. I walked out of the supermarket one day, and I was like, Wow, the Wasatch Mountains look so different from what you see anywhere else. It just caught me by surprise. Eight years in, and they're still doing that. Utah is unlike any state that I've ever lived in or been to. You can definitely make your mark here, even if you've only been here for a short amount of time.

" You can definitely make your mark here, even if you've only been here for a short amount of time. "

—ALYSSHA (DAIRSOW)

JAMES: *Meligha, you're a good example of that, coming into a high-profile position at the Black Cultural Center at University of Utah a couple years ago. Your journey to Utah was a little different. Can you share some of that with us?*

MELIGHA: So I'm originally from Rochester, New York. I came here through New Mexico. I was in the Army for a couple years—in Las Cruces, southern New Mexico. It was a small college town where I attended New Mexico State and worked as a coordinator in the university's Black programs. Coming out here was kind of a cultural shock, because even New Mexico is a minority majority state. And this [Utah] is the complete opposite, where things that I was taught as far as diversity initiatives haven't happened here before.

So you get the struggles of coming from the East Coast originally and people kind of just being always real. I came from a place where people were just raw and would tell you how they really feel. Here, I think the culture overall is a little more passive–aggressive, but it's still been a good transition. It's very political, but also high-profile, even though I don't necessarily think of it as such. The university itself is in its own place — or, as they used to call it, the place on the hill. A lot of people in the community look to the university for what they represent. Essentially, the question is: How do you make sure that it's accessible, particularly to Black folk? It's been a challenge, but a good one. I don't think I'd be able to do this everywhere in the country. There are several jobs that are similar to mine across the country, but I really think that I'm able to shape something here, and I love it.

" There are several jobs that are similar to mine across the country, but I really think that I'm able to shape something here, and I love it. "

—MELIGHA GARFIELD

JAMES: *I remember when they introduced the concept of the Black Cultural Center at the University. It's a big change from when I was there and there was only a Black Student Union.*

MELIGHA: The Black Cultural Center is really a space to help faculty, staff, and students in the broader community that identify as African and are part of the African diaspora. It also is for the broader community that doesn't identify as Black to learn about Blackness overall.

We are culturally affirming educational initiatives. We do service. We also do research on all things Black. We try to provide conversations and to spotlight faculty members who may not get the attention they deserve, to help them share their research. Dr.

Charles Rogers does colon cancer research on Black men, or you have Dr. William Smith who developed the concept of Racial Battle Fatigue. We want to give them the platform and a voice to highlight things that may not necessarily be on the mainstream, as far as academics pertaining to Black folks.

On the student front, we do a lot of different things, including creating initiatives that retain Black men in college, and also Native American and Latinx. We have a lot of initiatives. We're launching something called Operation Success, a leadership program for students to work in the Black Cultural Center and also work on a project that tackles a larger issue not only in the world but also here locally. We're really excited about that.

Really, overall, we're just making sure that students, faculty, staff, and the community feel supported, and then on top of that, learn about Black history in Utah and in Salt Lake City. For some reason, it was just a spark for me here in Utah, of all the places I interviewed. Part of it was because it was an inaugural position. There was never a center before. All the other places that I applied to, their centers had been there for like thirty or forty years. I saw this as a challenge, and I like challenges. How can I shape this particular center and put a stamp on it—not necessarily just for myself, but really see what the community wants out of this? How can we work together to make sure that this is a success, so the university and also Salt Lake City doesn't forget about it?

JAMES: *You definitely are shaping something here. You both are. Alyssha, tell us a little about Curly Me!.*

ALYSSHA: So Curly Me! is my baby. It's a resource for families with girls of African descent, or black girls between the ages of five to fourteen years old. We hold quarterly events and group mentoring opportunities to help educate, empower, and encourage them to be their best selves. It definitely is a part of my journey in Utah, this whole stepping out on faith and getting out of my comfort zone, and it's challenged me throughout the years, starting in 2015.

Going to the level where I'm having these conversations with national and international companies when we're talking about funding opportunities, this has definitely been one of the best journeys I've ever been on. You don't know what the next day will bring, but what you provide to the community is appreciated and respected.

A multi-hyphenate who's built ongoing momentum for herself and her clients, Michelda is a passionate wealth advisor and personal banker and business specialist with Wells Fargo. She's also the founder of Versatile Image, a consulting organization she launched more than seven years ago. Through Versatile Image, she and her team use the arts as an avenue to inspire economic growth in Black and Brown communities. They also help startups, entrepreneurs, small business owners, and artists build a solid foundation that promotes the growth of their businesses and personal financial position.

JAMES: *I know you have lots to share, but I'm interested in hearing again about Versatile Image and its impact. It was a for-profit, and then you decided to go nonprofit, right? Tell us a little bit about that.*

MICHELDA: I'm just listening to what God told me, to be honest. About three years ago, I actually put Versatile Image on the shelf. I had become very passionate about financial literacy. I was starting my licensing and working at a financial firm. I was out doing workshops and community outreach and all that stuff.

I didn't know what direction I should take Versatile Image. I'd been doing it for so long and just felt like maybe I should put it away for a little bit. It was on the shelf for three years, and God was just like, *Turn it into a nonprofit.* When it was a for-profit, though, I was able to get myself out of debt, I was able to start building a little bit of a cash reserve, and I was able to really pour more into my clients. Honestly, branding and marketing is not cheap—and that's one of the core elements of a business that determines your ability to make a lot of money and whether people are going to take you seriously.

Black people were really struggling with paying for quality work, not just a logo that you put on a flyer, but something that they could use to build a brand identity. They were just really struggling to be able to pay for the services that come with marketing and branding, like a decent website, and so I would, out of pocket, kind of absorb the cost between me and the other person. Then I started eliminating my consulting fee. I didn't want to charge someone $250 to sit down and help them, so I eventually started doing things for free. So honestly, it just made sense to become a nonprofit. I really wanted to be a resource to our community in a way that we could provide this service to them, where they didn't feel it was breaking the bank. We do make sure that the people that we contract to help are majority Black and Brown also. So we connect them to Black and Brown graphic designers, web designers, business tax specialists—whatever they need.

JAMES: *Has it met your expectations for what you were trying to accomplish by turning it into a nonprofit?*

MICHELDA: It has exceeded my expectations. I was just going with what God told me to do. Once I did, the floodgates just opened up. People wanted to volunteer their time, their space, their talents. We have graphic designers on staff who do not charge us; they help us get a brand starter kit for these clients. If they need to do something more, then we would contract someone and they would have to pay a certain portion of it, and then we would absorb the cost for the rest. We think that it's important that we don't set the model of giving everything out for free. No, it's your business; you should invest in it—that's an important message.

Michelda speaking at a Black Lives Matter protest

What we will do is get you in contact with someone who does quality work, who is going to give it to you at a price that is reasonable. But after you go to phase two, you have to respect people's business like you want them to respect yours. We'll get you to a point where you're making enough revenue to then be able to pour some back into your business.

We're diving in and elevating the way that we market Black businesses, and that's another thing that makes Versatile Image unique: We're not waiting for anybody to come to us. We are going to do what we need to do to get our funding in place, and I'm working hard to know every single Black-owned business here in Utah.

JAMES: *I feel like a lot of times—and correct me if my perception is wrong—it feels like Black folks take such pride in what they do that it's hard for them to ask for help.*

MICHELDA: That's what capitalism actually kind of creates in America is like — self-made, blah, blah, blah. I want to know one business that didn't need a customer. To be able to make that money, you're not self-made, you know what I mean? So you put your business in a certain place in a community, because you know it's going to bring you money. So you should also respect those people who are there. So you're not self-made, per se, but that's the mentality that has been trickling through from generation to generation. For a lot of people, where we have nothing, and we're like, *No, we want to have something of our own*, that pride comes along feeling like protection. We also don't want to seem like we're not capable. If we at Versatile Image can show that we're just as invested in them as they are in us, and as the community that lives here is, I think that's going to make a big difference. Then we're able to connect with them, person to person.

The goal is to be able to help other people. How can we help you make that a reality with the Chamber, with the business development programs, etc.? We're going to get you in contact with the Chamber, they do X, Y, and Z, and we're going to help you make it happen. Then we'll get someone who specializes in what we want to be able to create, kind of like a blueprint like Jay Z says, "a business blueprint." There are going to be other Black organizations or businesses that we can funnel these people through where they feel safe, where they feel they're not going to be taken advantage of. That's not saying that all Black businesses have to worry about that with our white counterparts, but, historically, we have reason to have some reservations there. The truth is, honestly, ain't nobody gonna be invested in you like the

Black community. We're invested even in the white community, the Asian community, the Latinx community; we literally support everybody.

" The truth is, honestly, ain't nobody gonna be invested in you like the Black community. "

—MICHELDA GEORGE

JAMES: *That's what I love about our culture: We love elevating everybody.*

MICHELDA: We need to realize that within our own communities and start doing a lot more collaborative work. It was one of the things that was very frustrating moving out here: It felt so small. It's such a small Black community; I want to see us all work together. It wasn't that people want us to be the only Black or the first Black or just have their name on something. The bigger thing is, can we just work together? Because there is so much here where even if we grew to 5 percent, there's still a lot of wealth that can go around. We don't have to have a scarcity mentality.

JAMES: *So as you were growing this organization and getting more clients, you said you took a leave from Wells Fargo. Now you have Versatile Image and you're working to become a financial advisor. How are you doing all this, and what's life like for Michelda?*

MICHELDA: Michelda needs a little more sleep! I'm still on leave from Wells Fargo, and I am entertaining an opportunity to be a financial advisor. That's the next step. But I am really full-time at Versatile Image right now, but I'm also still working on me, still taking some time out to handle some things that push me back for a really long time.

JAMES: *I know you like to work multiple facets. As I'm learning within the Black community, we really have a hard time focusing on one thing. We love exploring all of our gifts and just putting it out there. But you know, you have the financial advisory passion, you have the Versatile Image passion, but is there one that outweighs the other?*

MICHELDA: That's a pretty tough question. I don't know if I'd be able to choose, and the reason why I say that is because I see them as both being equally important. For me, wanting to be a financial advisor is just the next step for my clients at Versatile Image. I want to be able to help them understand where to put that money and how to make it grow. I see both avenues as helping the Black community be able to acquire generational wealth—through ownership, with entrepreneurship, and being your own boss. For the financial literacy aspect of it, being able to help people actually put plans in place to maintain wealth, to manage it, to be able to know how to create a will and pass it on to the next generation is really an extension of what I do at Versatile Image. I want to be that safe place for them to know I've helped them make all this money, I also want to help them learn how to manage it and make it grow.

My one vision is to help Black people create generational wealth. It might be through a business, or it might be professional people or an average worker who just needs to know how to maximize their 401k or have their IRA outside of work. If I had to choose, it would be the financial side. Day in, day out, if I had to choose, that's what I would do. And I think that's part of the reason why I became very comfortable with turning Versatile Image into a nonprofit, because I really did want it to be a resource for the community. I needed it to be something that can live beyond me. If I'm not there, I still need this to be moving in a direction that makes sense. I'm really hoping I could do both forever, though.

JAMES: *Yeah. I was just curious if there's one that drives you more than the other, but there's this one vision that you have, and it takes both of them to accomplish it. Earlier, you were talking about the challenges of not only being a woman and a Black woman but also being a young Black woman in Utah striving to become an influencer here. What is the advice you would give to you Black women who are really ready to accomplish big things here.*

MICHELDA: Know yourself, know who you are as a person, and stand on that ground. It's easy to get lost with everything that goes on in any place where you live, but I feel like Utah is like a little unique. I always describe it to people as, like, living in *The Truman Show*. If you haven't seen that movie, watch it. I know my brother said that to me when I was going to move here, he said, "Know who you are before you move to Utah." And I'm grateful for that piece of advice, because it's true; you'll get lost in a lot of things, especially if you're a Black woman. We want to do a lot, and we're limited by so many things. Me being young, me being a woman, me being Black, me being in Utah. Even for the education portion, I haven't finished my degree yet, and there are people in Utah who assign a certain level of class when it comes to education and just wealth. It gives you access to certain people.

> " Know yourself, know who you are as
> a person, and stand on that ground. "

—MICHELDA GEORGE

So know yourself and, if you don't yet, be okay with discovering yourself in this space. Figure out who you are. Stand on that ground. Believe in yourself and just do what you got to do to get it done. But also always do right by people, and don't let people limit you. The way that I feel like I was able to get my name in people's ears is by exploring all my talents. I started off performing poetry, and then people found out about me. That's how I was circulating in so many different circles, because I explored my talents and I was just authentically being myself.

I'm super excited and honored to be part of the Black community here and looking to really pay homage to you and the other community leaders that have been here, like Miss Betty Sawyer, who's been here doing the work for years. I'm just coming in and trying to learn, trying to be a part of what you all have done, so that I can build on what is already established here.

A native of South Africa, Siya moved to Iowa as a child and eventually found his way to Salt Lake City. A thought leader in the spheres of technology, product management, and community building, he's an entrepreneur at heart, always watching for the next opportunity and finding new ways to connect with leaders in government and industry. He is also an investor in Salone Monet, a color-inclusive nude shoe brand that has served clients such as Beyoncé and Gabrielle Union and is Black woman-owned.

JAMES: *Siya, welcome. Share with us a little bit about how you came to be in Utah.*

SIYA: Well, we came here from Iowa first, because my mother wanted to advance her career with a PhD. So we get to Iowa from South Africa, and immediately, we get hit with culture shock as everyone does, socially but also academically. It just hits you on all levels in ways that Americans would never imagine. She was already very educated. She earned the first college degree not only on her side of the family but also on my father's side of the family.

She was a teacher, and then she became a lecturer at a university in South Africa, the same university that had, at that point, graduated the most African presidents and African heads of states. Nelson Mandela went there and the presidents of about fourteen countries.

When we got to Iowa, we were expecting to be there for three years. That's what we told my grandma. We're going to be here for three years and come back and then she'll get a different, better job. We get here and immediately they're like, "Your damn

Siya speaking at an event at the Capitol

credits aren't going to work." *Oh, wow.* "You need a second master's, and then you can get a PhD." So culture shock number one,
just issues in academia that you wouldn't think of.

Since then, it's been a constant push and pull of learning everything from the immigration system to academia, which is why
we came here. She ended up having to get a second master's and
then a PhD, which obviously took longer than three years.

We got here in 2000. I think she got a PhD in 2007. I come
from a divorced household, so we had to make that work. Need-
less to say, she's a strong lady. I always say, everywhere I moved,
I kept on being pulled by strong women. First was my mother
taking us to Iowa. And when I was in Iowa, I met a young lady
who was very well traveled, and she was finishing med school. She
matched to a residency program in Salt Lake City, Utah, which
I never dreamed of going to. That's what pulled me to Utah. So
my major moves in life have been because of some woman who's
important to me, one way or the other.

JAMES: *I imagine culture shock from Iowa to here wasn't as crazy as going from South Africa to Iowa.*

SIYA: What I appreciate about being here is seeing, like, how much the landscape changes from Iowa, the Midwest, to California. From Nebraska to the Badlands, the mountain of the West. You just go from Denver until you get to Phoenix and until you get to California, it all seems like a blur. But then you get here.

In what I expected, first of all, there are the obvious religious implications. This is a Mecca for an entire religion, right? Everyone asked me about the same thing. You get here, and it's very much part of the historical context of how this place is formed, but I was also surprised to find this is the friendliest place for immigrants to be. I would have never guessed that's what you'd find here, in the middle of the Mountain West. Very much the culture of how the church ended up here, with persecution, feeds into what the policy ends up being. So with the intersectionality of me being Black but also me being an immigrant, I very much appreciate that. When I met the governor for the first time, I made it a point to personally thank him for that. In the middle of all this political turmoil, where immigration is a hot topic, and it's very divisive, he was like, "Let's take more immigrants." He got to the White House in the middle of all of it. That's Utah culture that's very specific to this place compared to every other state in the Midwest. With my story, I feel like there's a bit more empathy in this environment than anywhere else.

JAMES: *Yeah. We talk a lot about how Utah has always been an important resettlement area for refugees. But do you have a sense of why we're so welcoming for immigrants compared to other states?*

SIYA: I was actually discussing that with friends. I hear a lot of it, and I think it has to do with the folks who first settled here. They were Mormons who were religious refugees, for lack of a better term. I'm not a scholar on this, but they were fleeing persecution from the rest of the country to find some way to make a place that can be their own. So embedded in the founding story of this Zion, Salt Lake City is very much the story of people looking to find their home away from something they had to get away from, to create a new identity. So I think very much part of the culture of the place is being always open and welcoming. At least that's my sense in the three years that I've been here. And then—not to stay too much on the religious and social aspects—but there's a rite of passage in the faith: You have people going on missions. So it's a community that has more international ambassadors compared to other places. Just by virtue of missions, there are people who speak different languages, languages from all over the world.

They got experiences from all over the world, and they took them back here with them. So I imagine what it feels like for a bunch of people from all over the world when they come here and find someone that understands them or at least knows where they're coming from. Language is another thing I wouldn't have guessed we'd find—so many languages that have been spoken by immigrants, refugees, and the people who've been on missions. Of course, to quote Mandela, if you speak so a man understands you, you speak to his head, but speak in a man's mother tongue, and you'll be speaking to his heart. Even if there's no cultural understanding back and forth, if someone speaks in a language that you have spoken your whole life, you're immediately more comfortable in that space.

JAMES: *Was there a moment when you arrived here in Utah, where it was like, what am I doing here in Salt Lake City? And then what was the point where you felt like you could get down with this place?*

MIYA: By the time I left, I hadn't done anything in entertainment, economic development, or international and community development. I just enjoyed connecting people in the arts and promotion there and bringing together some concerts. For me, it's just about connecting with people from all over the world, Iowa to the rest of the world at a show called "Homeland to Heartland." The basic idea was to build a bridge of starting a conversation rather than being standoffish. I had done all that stuff, but it wasn't until the last year of redoing that show that I was able to get the mayor to come on my show. Maybe it was part of my growth that when I got here, I knew what I was capable of. I was ready to walk into City Hall and talk to economic development directors. For the most recent mayor, I met her right on the campaign trail. At the end of this event — it was, I think, her first town hall meeting — we ended up chatting for like forty-five minutes, just hitting it off and sharing different perspectives. What I got from all those experiences is a whole bunch of people that understand the lack of diversity here, who agree we need to face it head on and be open to ideas about what we should do about it.

They're waiting for people who are going to come either with ideas or who are going to be proactive about writing this new chapter, a one hundred-year history of diversity. I just found a lot of reception in government and in business in the startup community. Technology is still a tough cookie. A lot of that stuff is just systemic. In any industry, we could talk about everything from the financial industry to the technology industry to even government where you go, *No one looks like me here*. But when you show up, no one is giving you the cold shoulder and closing the door in your face. All of that is impossible to know until you actually show up to the door.

JAMES: *How were you able to get to those doors in the first place?*

MIYA: The same way I reached out to you. If you remember, I just reached out to you on LinkedIn and said, "Let's have coffee." You find a way to make yourself stand out and then actually make yourself part of the story of being in this place. Everybody deserves opportunities to be seen, or to be heard. That's a positive. You should use that as a fire to feel like, *I belong here*. Even if you look around and you don't feel like you belong in any given space, because equality was not created with you in mind, you need that fire. By the same token, nobody owes you nothing. So you deserve it—and nobody owes you. The only bridge between those two is you actually showing up.

> " So you deserve it—and nobody owes you. The only bridge between those two is you actually showing up. "

—SIYA MALI

You have to act like other people are going to be glad you showed up. Once you do show up, that other person will be open to ideas for involving you in whatever they've got going on. So I think for anyone who wants to be in power, that's an approach to take. That maybe also is just my personality, but I would also say a bunch of people, different generations that had different experiences here, will say that's what worked for them. So you kind of create your own story. I'm constantly told by people, "Man, if you were here five years ago. This is such a different place now." I hear that all the time, and all that communicates to me is the same thing I know about technology and the startup world, which is, everything is in transition. When everything is in transition, and it's just chaos everywhere, you have an opportunity to add whatever your vision is. It's a chance to bring your own unique perspective, stand by it, be ready to be corrected if you're wrong and learn from it, and learn from other people.

That's just the nature of the world, seven-plus billion of us around here. I find my people.

JAMES: *I love that mindset. The main thing that stuck out to me is that you did take this by the horns; you went out and started meeting people, realizing that Utah, overall, has an open-door policy.*

SIYA: I'm sure you talk to community leaders, Black leaders from all over the nation. You've got to put in some time to get some meetings, right? If Salt Lake is a top 30 city in America, the top 25 has nobody answering your call or taking your meeting unless he knows you.

You're not going to find too many places as open as it is here. You're not going to find it in Denver. Even in the Midwest, you're not going to find that in Phoenix. You will not find that in LA unless you're specifically plugged to a specific industry and those specific relationships. So it's been really cool so far, and I'm only three years deep, getting ready for my first children's play.

JAMES: *Congrats on that. You've only been here for three years, maybe skipping one year as a blip because of COVID, and already you've been networking in a lot of spaces, meeting a lot of different people.*

SIYA: My personality is all about exploring. I just show up to the door. When you are sincere about your approach, people tend to respond to that. So God bless whoever gets to read this book. Hopefully, all this support can be maintained, especially by Black folks who are here already, so the next generation can feel like a bunch of people looked out for them. I definitely owe it to whoever comes in next to at least give the lay of the land.

JAMES: *So do you consider this your forever place?*

SIYA: My wife and I have talked about that, and we think of this as long-term. For her career, when she gets done with her residency as a surgeon, she'll have to go somewhere for a fellowship for at least a year or two. We were talking about whether we'll come back and talking about home ownership versus renting. I feel like, *let's build equity in a home.* I want to hold onto that. If we're going to be gone, we can rent that space for a year or two. For the long-term question, it is absolutely in the cards, but we'll definitely be here for four more years and looking to create as much of an impact as possible.

JAMES: *So let's dig into your impact in terms of your profession. You've been talking about startups and technology. Is that your space?*

SIYA: I think there's an exciting opportunity globally in this new economy that is being built, and it crosses so many things by the scalability of it all. I've always been jealous of Black Americans. Just like the late, great Paul Mooney said—and I'll edit it: Everybody want to be Black, but nobody want to be Black. I mean the classics, jazz, hip-hop, the style—everything. Everyone sees the result of what produces Black Americans without seeing the struggle. Hip-hop, for instance, was born out of Black communities being starved, right? They took away instruments. They stopped funding arts programs. All they had was turntables. Now hip-hop is the most commoditized culture imaginable since rock and roll.

I don't think we have that crossover for technology yet. Probably everybody reading this knows TikTok or Twitter and knows Black Twitter and Instagram. Black people haven't been part of upgrading it. We might not have the distribution right now, but the artistic development, the strategy, the vision for certain artists we all consider iconic—that's where it's going to come from. What is the Motown of technology? It'll be a damn shame in ten years if we still don't have that. If I'm able to get behind something like that, to put Black folks into that technology space, that's where I want to be. You have an iPhone in your pocket with at least thirty apps. Every one of them is a company that was founded by someone with a unique perspective. You can do it, too, and not only can you but you should because of your very unique perspective and all the ways we act and behave as a culture. That should be owned instead of copied and appropriated. That's where I get excited, and that's the opportunity I see in startups and technology.

SIX

Utah Native

Growing up Black in Utah, I felt like I lived two separate lives at times. I didn't realize until I was an adult that I was "code switching." When you're learning to adapt to an environment where you're the only one most of the time, you find yourself speaking or acting a certain way to be accepted or included in situations. It's not until I go to a church function or service where I feel like I can be myself because I was around people where I felt understood. I had two sets of friends, LDS and non-LDS, because my non-LDS friends couldn't do things like hang out on Sundays and Mondays. Some parents weren't really accepting of friends that weren't LDS, so we would only hang out at school or in big groups and organized activities.

Throughout my life, I learned how to navigate the Utah environment. Navigating Utah the way I learned is not challenging nor would I say it's required to live here. However, developing an understanding of the dominant community and the lifestyle it brings does give you an edge. Living in a place that doesn't have a lot of diversity, you'll learn there's more ignorance than there is racism, and if you establish a connection with them, it provides you an opportunity to educate. Sometimes it may require a little bit of patience and maybe even biting your tongue at times, but with the rapidly growing population, I take it as a responsibility in order to see more faces like mine.

Utah's population has grown so much over the last several years, people are surprised to discover Utah natives these days, especially from the BIPOC community. Very few of the people I regularly associate with today are natives. Back in the day, we didn't want to admit it. We just didn't want to answer all the questions we would get. "Are you LDS?" "There are Black people in Utah?" "Do you know Karl Malone?" "How racist is it there?" Instead, we would skirt around the questions and mention where our parents or grandparents are from. Although we were born here, we weren't really proud to represent our hometown. Utah is known sometimes as being in its own "bubble." People outside are not too familiar with the state other than knowing it's the home of the LDS Church and skiing, and people inside Utah feel their state is a few years behind the rest of the country as far as trends and culture, especially those which impact people of color. When traveling outside of Utah, you prepare yourself to respond to the questions being asked about Utah and if you're part of the LDS church. You also engage in experiences you hope Utah would adopt. When you're in a place that is majority Black, something you're not used to, it's different. The only experience similar is at church, but in a secular setting when the minority is the majority, it can be a little uncomfortable in the beginning. You hope you're able to fit in and not "act like a Utahn."

Utah is becoming more comfortable for people of color, but it does still take time for residents to adjust. I take responsibility as being an ambassador for Utah. I know Utah is a welcoming state.

Yes, we are a little different. We have our diversity challenges. Yet, I'm excited for our future. The opportunities are presenting potential I didn't see us ever having. I can truly say now I am a proud Utah man, even though I still prepare myself when traveling out of state.

A senior mortgage specialist at Christian Roberts Mortgage, Mikell Brown has built more than ten years of experience in mortgage lending. After leaving sales and the cellular industry, Mikell launched his career in mortgages by focusing on government-sponsored loans. He also learned to navigate HUD so he could help any client create the opportunity to buy a home. He's now an expert in conventional, Jumbo, VA, FHA, HARP, and many other types of government programs. Active in the community, he serves on the board of the Utah Black Chamber as vice chair and works to help the organization grow. He married his high school sweetheart, Stephanie, and they have two daughters.

JAMES: *First, let's start with your area of expertise. As Salt Lake City has grown, so has the cost of homes. Do you have recommendations about affordability or maybe the best place for people migrating to Utah to look for homes?*

MIKELL: It depends on their stage of life. Are they single? Or if they're married with kids, they are going to try to gravitate a little bit more to the city center and start there and then maybe branch out depending on what their budget is. There are still affordable condos and smaller places throughout the city; it just really depends what you're looking for. People who are relocating with families like places like South Jordan and Bluffdale because you're getting a little bit more bang for your buck there. The houses are a lot bigger, and there are going to be other kids around.

I have two clients who just came in from California—one from Southern California who has two kids so they're moving down to Sandy, but they were raised here so they already like that area. The Avenues is always a hot spot. Another hot, hot market I think that will continue to appreciate is going to be the Rose Park, Taylorsville, Murray areas. I think that's where a lot of the gentrification will come from, and probably the next time the city puts a little bit more redevelopment dollars into it, I can see that whole area changing.

JAMES: *When you talk about gentrification, that reminds me of something I wanted to ask. The recent statistics came out on Utah's diversity. One thing that caught our attention is that Black homeownership was so low. What do we need to do as a community to fix that?*

MIKELL: Number one is education. What I find out a lot of times, especially with younger people trying to enter into the homeownership game, is that they're not entering because they're waiting to be established. They just don't think it's the right time, but what they may not know is there are a lot of programs out there to help you get into a house for little to no money down. There's a great program called Utah Housing, where they subsidize the down payment with just basically a second mortgage. A lot of people look at what they can afford, their credit, and other questions they ask themselves rather than doing the research to really verify where they are.

They end up going to rent an apartment when they could possibly be owning a house for $300 a month and also building equity. When the market pushes like it has over the last couple of years, they can actually walk away having made a return on their investment—that's often true even if you're staying here for just a few years.

JAMES: *With so many opportunities in the tech sector and others where you have higher salaries, do you feel like we still have affordable housing? Or where's the balance?*

MIKELL: I think there's still a market for affordable housing, and I think there's more effort from the city and county governments to try to make it available. But also, some of the homeownership aspects that I want to talk to people about are sacrifices within your own budget. Can you afford a house? How can you put together a specific plan to be able to go ahead and get into that? How do you save? Yes, there's going to be affordable housing, *how* affordable is the question. I don't think people are getting priced completely out of the market, but it is getting close. The thing that I've been able to see doing mortgages is you get a macro look at everybody's finances, people from every walk of life. There are always going to be those opportunities for further affordable housing.

JAMES: *Okay, so let's transition to the reason people hopefully are looking to buy here. What are some things you get excited about here in terms of the landscape of Utah's community, the Black landscape in particular?*

MIKELL: Just the growth of the community, for one. I like to see the diversity within our own group. So many people are moving here, and the amount of diversity is increasing. We're not a monolith; right? You always hear that, *Black people are not a monolith.* We're going to have Black Republicans out here; we're going to have Black Democrats out here; we're going to have Black alternative people that listen to different types of music. To see that group of people become more diverse—you know, Black, gay, and lesbian—to see the shift of that and to have all those people here and wanting the entire community to thrive, that's the most important thing to me overall. When you look at a Black person, they're not going to be this specific way, or this specific type of the way that we're portrayed in the media. I was talking to Nikki Walker, and she was saying some of the most bougie people she's met are Black people. Why can't we embrace that? Those are going to be the people who are going to be able to help lift our community. It's the same idea as being part of the chamber. We'd like to see so many Black businesses investing in the chamber because we give a lot of support. I would like to see that support coming from our community as well.

" To see that group of people become more diverse—you know, Black, gay, and lesbian—to see the shift of that and to have all those people here and wanting the entire community to thrive, that's the most important thing to me overall. "

—MIKELL BROWN

JAMES: *Absolutely. Having more Black businesses and bigger businesses that are keeping us moving allows us to reinvest that, basically creating our own ecosystem.*

MIKELL: I think that's true with every community, and it's not that we're trying to leave out any other communities. It just always seems like if you don't care about your community, or you don't care about yourself, who else is going to do it? With our chamber, we've always been super inclusive. That's part of our mission.

JAMES: *Agree. So, as a native, what stands out to you about how the community is changing?*

MIKELL: Even seeing the change over the last ten years from my previous thirty years here, it's just been amazing. You're starting to see the culture shift, not only here in Salt Lake, though that's where the epicenter has always been in terms of being more liberal and changing faster. We high Utah counties are starting to branch out a little bit more, and I'm just embracing that. Now we're getting a lot more cultures; our Asian and Indian communities are growing rapidly because of the tech industry.

I'm excited to see what that's going to bring to Salt Lake and Utah as a whole in regards to restaurants, different types of entertainment, things like that. You know, one day I took my dogs out to a dog park and I saw some people playing cricket in the middle of a park on a Sunday. I've never seen cricket played before in my life. That's the type of change, even little things like that, that will change the environment and change the culture.

JAMES: *It does seem like there are pockets where you can go, maybe, five minutes away, and the landscape changes and becomes less or more diverse.*

MIKELL: When you're talking to people, it's like, where are the majority of Black people? People expect, in our Western world, that this is where you'll find a lot of Hispanics. Black families are remote because we're so spread out, but navigating it as a whole is always hard. In my neighborhood, sometimes if you don't make a concerted effort, you might not see others in that area, even at a store or anything like that. It's hard to navigate sometimes, but for the most part, my neighborhood is pretty good, and I've come to love areas close to the mountains. I started to spend a lot more time outdoors—snowboarding, golfing, things like that. Then it's just as close to the central nucleus of Salt Lake, so I could jump on the freeway and be anywhere throughout the city.

JAMES: *You do live in a beautiful area. You mention this quick jump to the canyons. I'm curious, did you start exploring the outdoors as an adult? Or did you always?*

MIKELL: It's funny, the first time I ever went snowboarding, I was twenty-six. I started in Lake Tahoe, and it was a guy's trip with my cousins. We were going snowboarding and skiing. I was twenty-six-years-old, and they're like, "Man we every time we came and visited you"—because they're from California—"we were skiing or snowboarding." I lived here and never went, but my dad was just never really into that portion of it. I've learned a lot over the last eight to ten years, mostly being in the area that I'm in. I really became passionate about snowboarding, and I'm trying to integrate more people into it as they come into town.

Mikell Brown posing after snowboarding

I have definitely become an outdoorsy person. I like being able to use ATVs or go out to explore our mountains. We have five national parks in Utah within a few hours. It would be such a loss to come out here and not enjoy the beauty. People from Europe plan trips here for a week or two and travel halfway around the world for what we have in our backyard. To not take advantage of places like Arches and Moab is a shame. It's just so beautiful, and you can get anything within a couple hours. It's pretty amazing. There's the one thing I think that Utah always has to offer is that people here are willing to share the gems with you. If you want to go camping, I'm sure there's somebody in a group that you know who will show you the way and show you some special spots that you can enjoy.

JAMES: *Everybody wants to help everybody here, and I realize, through these interviews, how good we have it here. So what was it that shifted your mindset to wanting to do more outdoor stuff? Was it just that family visit? What really got you?*

MIKELL: Different groups of friends. I have friends who golf, friends who like to hike, friends who snowboard. It's just really diversifying the people I'm around for the most part. I've always been willing to do pretty much anything when it comes to activities. Now my kids are enjoying it too. My daughter's love camping. They definitely love the mountains and skiing. I've learned along with them. I got them in ski lessons, and they're pretty good. They can actually go out and be by themselves on the mountain, and I feel safe about it. They definitely embrace it, and now we have friends with kids who love to do the same activities.

One of the region's most successful real estate agents, Kellen Perkins, comes from a long line of thriving Utahns. After a brief attempt at living elsewhere, he returned to his roots as a young man and built a life and career here, following in his ancestors' footsteps. He's also a strong advocate for the LGBTQ+ community, having served as a volunteer at the Pride Center as a teenager, enjoying the support he found among friends, family, and the community as a whole.

JAMES: *Good to see you, Kellen. One thing that stands out to me is that when I graduated high school, most of my friends left town. You didn't. What kept you here?*

KELLEN: Family kept me here. I left the mountains for a little bit, but I came back. I grew up in Salt Lake City, ten minutes from a trail. I biked all over downtown. When I left, I moved to Scottsdale, Arizona. They have hills; they don't have mountains. It was nice to come back. As I hit adulthood, my grandmother, who was my primary caregiver, passed away. I spent my early to mid-twenties in quite a bit of mourning. It was like I had to be around family in order to survive.

JAMES: *That's what a lot of folks say. When they stay, it's often because of family and the family environment.*

KELLEN: You know, I've traveled all over the world. I stay ready. I'll book a flight right here, during this conversation, and be gone this evening. But I really do love being here. I love being around my family. I've hosted dinner parties and all sorts of stuff in my home, taking over where our parents left off.

JAMES: *I know there's a lot of history here for your family, too. This year or last year, there was a street named after one of your family members, right?*

KELLEN: That was Samuel Chambers, and it's in Mill Creek where the new Mill Creek Center is going to be built. Samuel Chambers was a farmer. If you remember in seventh grade Utah history, you learned about our family but only in the context of slavery, freed slaves. They didn't talk too much about the business ownership or the farming part or the part where our family fed the community and was well respected within the community. They skipped over all of that in history class.

So Chambers was in Mill Creek. Green Flake's homestead was out in Fort Union, where Trader Joe's is. During those times, this was all considered the country. That's why they gave us our forty acres and a mule and put it out there. They never thought that it would expand to what it is now, right? Now it's some of the most desired real estate in the whole state. Chambers and his wife were farmers in the late 1800s. Green Flake was one of my great grandfathers.

JAMES: *So tell us about why you did leave briefly after high school?*

KELLEN: My brother had been to Scottsdale. I spent my childhood going back and forth. My siblings are significantly older than I am, so I spent my childhood visiting. My brother had a business out there, and I went out to help, but I soon realized it wasn't going to work. I wanted to come back. I have deep, rich friendships here as well as family, and I was also coming out as queer during that time. My coming out experience happened around the Pride Center. I was a youth volunteer there, so I just felt a sense of community.

JAMES: *That's great. When people think about Utah, they think about it being a very conservative state. Many people do not know how welcoming it is for the LGBTQ+ community.*

KELLEN: Right now, it's incredibly welcoming. I think the issue we have is the intersection between the LDS church and LGBTQ, because those individuals do struggle with certain issues when it comes to their coming out process. You know, the proclamation of family and the ideals that are there. Whereas, for my upbringing, I grew up in a home that was diverse—ethnicity, race, religion. I grew up with Methodist and Baptist and Mormon, and the influence of Judaism, so I did experience all of that in my household. That allowed me to come out through my own process. Even when I did come out, I have a very religious Baptist uncle who was a preacher who said, "I don't think you're gay." Then he followed it up with, "I still believe that we all sin, we all fall short of the glory of God, and your sin is no different than mine and so whoever you become, I'm going to support." As I've gotten older, he's been one of my largest allies, through life in general. Family, spouse, everything. I've had that support. I think when you have a loving and supportive family, coming out and being who you are is a lot easier. My friends who had supportive families, even LDS families who were supportive, they thrived.

JAMES: *So you have the sense of community not only within your family but also externally as well. You mentioned the Pride Center and being a volunteer there. I've seen a couple of Pride festivals here, too. It seems like all of that is relevant.*

KELLEN: Yeah. I'm thirty-eight years old. I went to my first Pride festival at sixteen. When I came home, my grandma and mom would have a conversation saying, "Kellen, no." I had an advocate that

Kellen hiking in southern Utah

would drop me off at the Pride Center because it was before I was driving. My family there was loving. I found friendships and started volunteering and probably did that for three or four years until I started with my career.

JAMES: *Has that experience impacted your career at all?*

KELLEN: It's been really great. Having the sense of community that I have, I've built my business on relationships, all word of mouth, which has been very helpful. I don't do the same advertising a lot of people do. I didn't have to jump on the phones, right? When I started in real estate, I had built a community, and I'm building bridges. A lot of people thought that I would be a good resource. So yeah, it's been very helpful, and I'm always grateful.

JAMES: *And you've been in real estate for about ten years now, right? What got you wanting to do real estate?*

KELLEN: I grew up around it. My grandma always used to say, "God bless a child that has his own." I had a few opportunities, and the house fell into my lap. I had a stepbrother who was going to leave the house. I had the cash to go ahead and take care of that. I took it over. I didn't want to hold it, though, which was a big mistake. At that point, I was just kind of scared. I ended up selling the property to the city, so they used it for their program of helping individuals get housing. So it all worked out. Then I bought about six other properties over in the West Park area, flipping those, and then I was in the medical field. My best friend helped me realize I'd had a passion for real estate since I was a kid. There were three things I loved: family, real estate, and cars. That's still the same. I just feel blessed that ten years later, I'm still here and one of the top realtors in the city.

JAMES: *That's great. Congratulations on all your success. Talking about building your business in real estate and building it on relationships, do you have a very diverse client base? Do you find yourself attracting a certain client base, being Black, queer, and Jewish—those intersectionalities there?*

KELLEN: I look at housing from this standpoint: Whether you're buying a $5 box or a $15 million mansion, you're a human who has a goal. I try to treat people that way. I try to help my first-time homebuyers who were disenfranchised who are just trying to get in the door; I try to help them succeed. Then I also help my hiring clients with their goals as well. Make it about the goal and about the goal of that person. I find that as something that speaks to me.

JAMES: *How have you seen the Black community grow, in your ten years of experience in real estate? How can we be better, or what things do you wish to see?*

KELLEN: I believe we need to focus on buying. We need to focus on getting in the door. As a person who loves cars, I started to realize early on that I was lucky enough to have an uncle who showed me what a car payment was and then showed me what a house payment was. I realized that housing was a lot more affordable. He was showing me that a car payment, which will always be on a depreciating asset, is always going to be there if you continually buy one. But if you pay your house off, you own a piece of property. It's going to get paid off, and then eventually, you might have others help pay it off.

I believe all young people should get in, but they need to learn the basics of the finances. If you look at our country as a whole, we have a huge disparity in Black homeownership, right? Those numbers continue going down. Our highest time of homeownership was actually during the Civil Rights Movement. You have a dream and you focus and you keep working towards that. If you've lived from crisis to crisis to crisis, though, you lack the ability to create that goal. You lose sight. So things like TVs, cars, tennis shoes, all that stuff becomes more tangible and within reach. They're a value system; they're not about wealth building. Homeownership is wealth. For example, I bought a house at twenty-eight. I sold it two years ago for a $250,000 profit. When I rolled that into another investment, I felt so blessed. I've owned commercial buildings, you know, and my biggest mistake was that I let some of that go too soon.

> " I believe all young people should get in, but they need to learn the basics of the finances. "

—KELLEN PERKINS

JAMES: *How do you think the real estate here compares to other parts of the country?*

KELLEN: There's definitely opportunity. It depends on what part of the country you're coming from, too. With the history of Utah, Blacks have generally experienced a middle class upbringing. We grew up more in homes that were owned by our families as opposed to how many people grow up in inner cities. But then you look at some parts of California, where if their family owned a property and sold it and then came here to set up camp, that's a different experience than coming here and being able to buy property for the first time, which is something a lot of people see as impossible.

For instance, my family, from the 1800s to now, owned land, and that created the pathway for generational wealth. Whether everyone took advantage of that or not is a different story, but that opportunity was there. When I grew up in a house that my family owned for seventeen years—my whole childhood—that means my mind was set on buying a house. I saw myself as being able to own a home because that's what I knew. I traveled extensively. I've spent time in the South, where I can pick up a house for the cost of a Honda, but there are families there who see that $25,000 as something that can't be done. They're still paying rent on a property because they haven't had that generational wealth, and they haven't had the opportunities shown to them.

JAMES: *I've never thought about it that way. When we talk about opportunities here in Utah, one of the things that never comes up is generational wealth. We have had multi-generations of Black families, going all the way back to the pioneer days. Now many people are migrating from all over. So for those who are coming in fresh, without that background of having ancestry here, what other opportunities do you see here for those people?*

KELLEN: Well, if you're coming in with a new job, it's likely one of the newer professions that comes with a higher income level than those who've been here for generations. You have access to different upcoming areas. There's the possibility of getting in the door there already. On a condo, if you're a young individual coming in, you can pay $200 a month for rent for a two-bedroom downtown, or you can buy something twenty minutes away and pay the same amount and have three to four bedrooms. You have to think of it that way. It doesn't work for everyone, but if you can see yourself here for five or more years, get in on the growth while you're here.

While he's not a Utah native, Byron Russell has a valuable perspective that natives might otherwise take for granted. Shaped by his upbringing in Washington, DC, and his adventures around the world, he's worked to build the existing arts and cultural opportunities in Utah while still appreciating Utah's built-in amenities: the great outdoors. In Chapter 3, he discussed his thoughts on how to introduce children to the joys of art. Here, he shares why he believes the Black community needs to emphasize that these natural resources exist for us to enjoy as well.

JAMES: *You talked earlier about how much Utah has to offer in terms of the arts and quality of life. How do you feel that culture is built for us as Black individuals?*

BYRON: A lot of people move here because they embrace this idea that you can make your family a priority. Quality of life is really your capacity to live the life you want to live. If you decide you're going to raise a family in an environment that actually brings the joy of nature, this place provides it. People make a choice, right?

There are metropolitan areas, like New York, LA, San Francisco, or Atlanta. A lot of companies come here because they know their employees have families, and it's certainly a great place in comparison to others. If you're going to choose a place to raise kids and you really do want to find that balance of either being somebody within a business or corporate environment — or if you want to be an entrepreneur — I think there's a space for that.

I mean, think about people who have to be in LA, and they

drive for two hours. Or if you're in New York, and you live in a reasonable place, maybe in New Jersey or Connecticut, you're going to spend four hours of your life in transit every day. And, you know, there's one thing that that pandemic has taught us is that the quality of time that we have matters. I think that Utah has already been ahead of that curve, right? We have those freedoms with our time that other people don't have in different communities.

A lot of our Black Americans are not enjoying or don't think they have access to national parks and amazing space. I mean, my example was living in Washington, DC, being able to enjoy the Smithsonian, from the Air and Space Museum to the Black History Museum. As a Black kid growing up, I thought that was for white folks to go and understand and enjoy. At some point, I realized, *Wait, that's ours.* We belong there.

Once you feel that, you begin to experience something that is really meant for every single person, not just one culture or one race. I think the same thing is the case with natural spaces. What child would not go to Yosemite National Park or Yellowstone or to Zion National Park and not see beauty? I mean, it's in front of you.

Our national parks, arguably, are everyone's, though Indigenous populations feel that land was theirs. Having said that, I think that that's one thing our country got right, which was to make sure these spaces were there to be enjoyed, for generation after generation after generation. Open space, the beauty and grandeur that was created, for all of us to see for generations to come, is something that I really want more Black and Brown folks to experience, for them to recognize that this is ours. It's for your kids, and it's for your family, and it's for others ahead of you.

Most of the people who visit the parks are not necessarily

people of color, there are a lot of people from different countries who come and see this natural beauty. I think that's one of our roles, to inspire people to recognize that it's ours. It's all of ours.

" I think that's one of our roles, to inspire people to recognize that it's ours. It's all of ours. "

—BYRON RUSSELL

JAMES: *That's a great perspective, because for a lot Black Americans, we would never consider the outdoors as our, right? Because we were never introduced to it or never experienced it. We were people that grew up in the South or in a metropolis like Chicago, Atlanta, or New York. Yet, Utah, what we really promote is our outdoor experience, which doesn't attract a lot of people of color, right? How would we continue the same type of advertisement to bring people to Utah? How would you frame it?*

BYRON: It could be education. It doesn't necessarily have to be part of a curriculum, but why wouldn't you take a field trip to a place like Zion National Park or Bryce National park? You know, when I was back East, I remember taking a fellowship field trip to Williamsburg and learning about our nation's founding. That made me interested later in life to explore more of that, and to go to Monticello and to go to Mount Vernon. I think any parent would want to join in on that fascination that a child has. A parent doesn't have the same passion for an Xbox, but at the same time, they'll buy it because their kid wants it. So why not expose them to something that they can enjoy together?

It can be the same experience with art. I am a firm believer, and one of the reasons I really thought the Zoo, Arts & Parks campaign was so important is because the arts were not meant for the elite. As a young man, I went to Europe for the first time, and I was just fascinated by what I saw. The beauty. I don't know about Titian's technique, or the School of Raphael, or any of that. I just see something that looks beautiful. I came back, went to college, and took courses in architecture and art. And it absolutely blew my mind. It fascinated me. As I became more interested, I would have my mom come with me to the museum in DC. My mom, who raised me, had never been in the National Gallery. She began to say, this is something amazing. I've missed this. So I need to take my nephew, for example, my brother's son, and continue introducing this to my family.

We need to bring alive this passion and skill and desire for people. We need to make it available and not make it seem as if it's only for one culture, one community, one income, or one race.

SEVEN

Raising a Family in Utah

U tah is a great place to raise a family. Many people migrate to Utah for that reason. It's clean, safe, and environmentally structured to support families. For much of this, you can thank the foundation of the Church of Jesus Christ for Latter Day Saints. It's culture was structured for larger families. It's not uncommon to see families with four or more children. Utah is also the youngest state in the country because of the number of children per family. According to the most recent data, one out of ten people in Utah are less than the age of five, and the average age is twenty-seven years old. My parents were young when they welcomed their first child into the world. However, they were hardly alone in doing so. When I had friends return from their LDS mission, it was soon after they were married with a child on the way. It is not surprising to find three generations in sixty years.

Growing up, it was normal for me to be the "only one" in the class through grade school. Being the only one led to many interesting questions about my hair, skin color, and sometimes even how I spoke.

Kids will be kids, and they are curious, meaning no harm, but it was uncomfortable at times. It wasn't until high school that the Black student population was larger, and I had many kids I could relate with.

Today, Utah has several schools where the minority is the majority. However, many of the schools with a large minority population are also the schools in less affluent neighborhoods. It's a challenging conversation when a new Black family moving to Utah contacts the Black Chamber seeking to learn where to best relocate and where are the best schools. Of course parents want the best education but also hope to place them in an environment with peers that relate. How do you find the balance?

In addition, there's the challenge with connecting with other Black families. One of the great aspects of Utah's demographics is that you won't find pockets of certain communities in cities. Everyone is spread throughout. Everybody is welcome anywhere. It was only just recently, West Valley City, a city in Salt Lake County, the minority population became the majority. The minority population in West Valley is a mix of all minorities—Black, Hispanic, Asian, and Pacific Island.

In a state with a small diverse population, however, not having a "hub" presents challenges in connecting with one's community. When people arrive in Utah, they hope to have the community they came from. It's imperative they find a connection to their new community, otherwise they begin to feel isolated, alone in their efforts to do what's best for their family. Consequently, Utah becomes a stepping stone for them as they look for their next home.

While companies elevate their efforts to grow and retain their diverse talent with employee resource groups and other programs, employees are left alone after they leave the office to connect to their community. If you're a native to Utah, or have been a resident for a significant amount of time, you learn how to navigate and "find your tribe." It is not as evident to new residents. How do Black families find each other? If you're new to Utah, where does one go to find families that relate your background and experiences—to teach you how to adapt to this new place? How do you keep your children engaged and connected to your culture in a non-diverse community? How do you help them navigate the experience of being the "only one?"

In this chapter, you'll learn from families native to Utah, who have been here for several years, and from a couple who only started their family a few years ago. The future of any community lies in the foundation of its youth. The Utah Black Chamber can proudly say, Black Utah has a bright future.

Practitioners at Planted Healing Mental Health Practice and co-founders of Continuum Mind Body Collaborative, Melanie and France Davis focus on providing healing, encouraging Black representation among healthcare and mental healthcare providers, and creating spaces that connect and uplift people of color in Utah.

JAMES: *You spoke with us earlier about working in healthcare, breaking barriers, and launching practices and businesses in Utah. You're very busy, and that's all on top of raising children. Tell us about what it's been like for you, raising three children in Utah and raising them while you're both so involved in mental health and healthcare.*

FRANCE: We have three very active children. One of them is extremely active, a daredevil. He could hit a wall and bounce off it. I used to practice orthopedic surgery, spine surgery, and I know what he shouldn't do. On the mental health side, I know what concussions do to people. We probably give more restrictions as parents, because we know what's coming. We're always telling them about the statistics, always focusing on giving them tools to be successful. It's all the potential risks, which we know and think about.

There are a lot of conversations that happen in our house that may be unique, and we're pretty open with parenting. There are not many secrets around. We try to create a space where all kinds of conversations can happen. So we talk openly about mental health, community issues, and social justice issues.

Raising three Black children in Utah, we've learned what spaces are "safe" and what spaces are healthy and can help children thrive. We do, to some degree, try to create a pathway for our children with fewer barriers. We know there are certain things that happen here in our community. As much as it's trying to grow, there are still things in place that we'd like for any children to not have to experience. So, for us, it's about reducing certain risks, such as reducing our kids' exposure to untrained adults who have access to them in educational spaces. We try to really be very intentional about parenting, because it is so unique to parent Black children in Utah. We see the differences with some of our best friends who are raising children. The things that we teach our kids about and talk to our kids about, these other parents wouldn't even think about preparing their children for or educating their children about.

JAMES: *Here at the Utah Black Chamber, we get calls all the time from people moving to Utah who have kids and want to know what to expect. They are told this is a great spot for families. What would be your response?*

MELANIE: I'm mindful of the great efforts that are being made, but from my personal lived experience, which is all I can really speak from, you need to be really mindful of most of the schools that are not forwardly talking about equity, implicit biases in school, and are not educating their teachers about what those issues really mean.

In Utah, what I've seen as a child and family therapist is a lot of children who have been villainized in school systems, especially Black boys and Black girls, while the Black boys were often filtered into behavior modification plans. All of a sudden, somehow, every Black child has ADHD, which is not true. But that's the messaging that's being sent home, and that's what parents are responding to. When I hear those things, I say: "Oh, so is there racial trauma? Is this child experiencing different treatment from teacher to teacher, from preschool, to kindergarten, until third grade, and now it's coming out and they're struggling to sit still in school or focus?"

There are also fantastic public educators here in Utah who are trying to make many changes. I think they're making major moves in our community. Even they have acknowledged how far we have to go, though. So for us, because we wanted our children to have an experience that is a positive one, where they feel safe and loved, we found a school where the forefront of their mission is equity and embracing diversity. A place where this mission is a part of the curriculum. The teachers are sent to wonderful conferences, like the People of Color Conference, where they return with knowledge of the language of equity. I think as far as finding spaces, we found a private school downtown that has, built into the forefront of their mission, efforts to bring in different types of families, to have equitable education. You walk in and you see all types of pictures: Indian families, Asian American families, and Black families. It's in the literature and in the curriculum. It's inclusive, and our children really feel seen there.

JAMES: *Regardless of the ranking of the school, if the child is not confident that they can become who they truly want to be, they are not going to thrive in that environment. They need to be able to find their own niche. As Utah natives, what have you noticed that has been the biggest difference between your experiences growing up and your kids' experiences?*

FRANCE: I have noticed that the community of Black individuals is growing somewhat. I also think that, culturally, there were different interactions than there are now. When we were young, spending a lot of time in church was a big aspect of our lives, and that was where we would meet other children who shared our same culture. Now, even though we see that the population has grown, the community seems to be more spread out.

MELANIE: I do think that people are looking for ways to connect with different cultures. I see a lot of transracial adoptive families, which is the type of family I was adopted into and also how I ended up here in Utah. When I was younger, the only place there really was was Calvary Baptist Church. That was where I saw Black people. It was like the hub, right? Now, I see so much more diversity here. I see people online and in all of these different groups searching for spaces to connect. I'm not even a very religious person, but I see those spaces as safe places for my family. Church is almost an ideal rec center for my family. At church, we can come as we are, we can dance together, we can enjoy activities on the weekends, and we can see all of these amazing, positive, influential Black people.

JAMES: *So, you both have professions you could do anywhere in the country. What has kept you in Utah?*

MELANIE: I would say that even after living in quite a few places— New Jersey, DC, Kentucky, Indiana—I still find myself loving Utah, even though I see very clearly the things that need growth still. I think that the only factor that would be motivating enough to make us want to move would be the possibility of living some-where with more diversity, but it is still important to take into account your quality of life. We have friends who live in DC who are working like crazy; they don't see their families as much as we do, and we are super family-centered. Quality time with our kids is important in our family, and so is spending time with other family members. Both sets of our grandparents are here in Utah, and being able to spend time with them is important to us as well.

I think we originally moved back to Utah after France finished PA school because it was affordable. Then, when we started our family, it just felt so good to have a village of not only familiar faces like you but also our family and friends. We still have childhood best friends that we all that we grew up with. We enjoy the positive pace of our lives, and how we raise our children. Every day we go on walks in our neighborhood, and we scooter down for gelato or snow cones, and we know all our neighbors. That quality and type of life we are living has kept us here. In the last ten years, I would say the things that are important to me are food, fun things to do, the arts, and Utah is incredibly rich with fun new restaurants, the outdoors. All it's missing is Disneyland and the beach.

FRANCE: Another thing we love about Utah is that from here, you can easily travel to a variety of different places.

MELANIE: Honestly, our school has been a big part of it too. I think that one of the things that has been most influential in keeping us in Utah is our kids' school. There are so many systemic issues in the education system around the country; it doesn't matter where you live, there will still be issues. Because of the severity of these issues, we have grown to value this safe space we have found for our children in their school. Through this school, we have gained peace of mind when it comes to our kids' safety and care. To us, that is worth staying where we are. Even in a community that leaves much to be desired, as a family, you can create ways to enjoy yourselves, and even though the community may be lacking in some ways, it makes up for it in others.

FRANCE: And it's exciting to see the way it's growing. Employment opportunities are becoming much richer and more vibrant. We have tech companies coming into town, a hospital system that is growing, and all of the jobs that follow those growing industries. There's so much opportunity here.

" It's exciting to see the way it's growing. Employment opportunities are becoming much richer and more vibrant. We have tech companies coming into town, a hospital system that is growing, and all of the jobs that follow those growing industries. There's so much opportunity here. "

—FRANCE DAVIS II

BRANDON DAY AND
MICHELLE LOVE-DAY

Brandon and Michelle have called Utah home since 2005. A seasoned entrepreneur with a background in sales and marketing, Brandon has found welcome audiences for his endeavors in the area. Michelle, an educator, administrator, and now the founder of a new virtual academy, has discovered ways to connect with others in Utah's Black community and worked to make Black families, especially children, experience a sense of belonging. Between the two of them, they have five children, one son and four daughters, ages nine to twenty-two.

JAMES: *You two have been in Utah for around sixteen years so far, but you met in Vegas? Tell us a little bit about your story.*

MICHELLE: I was at a Delta Sigma Beta convention. I am from Ohio but living in North Carolina at the time. He was helping to work one of the events with a friend.

JAMES: *Brandon, where are you from originally?*

BRANDON: A little town with a population of one hundred in Star Valley, Wyoming. The only Black person in the entire valley and, I felt, the entire state. I was the only Black kid in elementary school, junior high, and high school.

JAMES: *So how did you two arrive in Utah?*

MICHELLE: So I was at the convention in Vegas for seven days. We talked and hung out and exchanged numbers. He had told me he was going to be moving to Utah. I was like, *I don't even know* *where Utah is.* I thought, *I'll never talk to him again.* Next thing I know, every day we would talk; before I went to work and after work, for four months, just on the phone talking. So finally, his birthday was coming up in December. We had met in July of 2004. I said, "Why don't you come out to North Carolina for your birthday?" This is before social media, so all I had was one grainy photo. He sent me another picture of him from Halloween, through email. He came out to visit for his birthday, and then that was it. I came to visit here in February for my spring break. Long story short, with me being an educator, it was easier for me to move than it was for him because he was with Hewlett-Packard at the time.

BRANDON: She started interviewing and had seven job offers by the end of the week. She realized very quickly that she would be a valuable commodity.

MICHELLE: I thought I'd move out here and see, try it. His kids were three and four at the time. Let's see if we can even have a relationship and let me meet the kids. They sealed the deal, once I saw how cute they were. They were very good kids. That was September of 2005. After I moved, on Memorial Day weekend, he asked me to marry him. That's my salesperson. He sold me this place, and I hadn't even heard of it before.

JAMES: *So, Brandon, from Wyoming to Salt Lake. How did that happen?*

BRANDON: So I went from Wyoming to New York City, if you can imagine that. I lived there for a while and then moved here. It was really just going to a job. Hewlett-Packard was hiring in Salt Lake. I had a friend who worked over here. It was in some ways like the area where I grew up. It's just kind of an easy place for people who grew up like I did to come to Salt Lake.

JAMES: *That makes sense. What was it like for you, Michelle, living in areas that were a little more diverse? How did you adapt to Utah?*

MICHELLE: Looking back, the first three years were a little difficult, some culture shock. It took me a while to adjust. Part of that was not seeing Black administrators for students. That's what actually pushed me to go back to get my second master's at U of U, so I could be a principal. I thought I was going to be a classroom teacher for the rest of my life, but seeing the lack of representation anywhere else at the upper levels in decision-making changed my trajectory. It was good professionally because it opened up my possibilities. My mindset changed to where I thought I was going to be happy wherever I moved.

BRANDON: I think, coming out here, she had to get involved with what was available. That's the great thing about Utah. There's so many things you can do. If you want to just go to the mountains and be by yourself, you can do it. It's beautiful. You can get away, but also she really got involved with theater, and there are some great theaters out here. She was able to find more people of color in theater, and also just created some really good friendships there.

MICHELLE: I went from literally just moving here to auditioning at the Hale Center Theatre. They had been doing a lot of good plays with Black folks. I think that helped unify my group. We were getting married, and I was doing this play, and it helped ground me. I'm still friends with those people to this day. To my surprise, I found one of my sorority sisters here. There's a chapter here. She had lunch with me when I was visiting. That was a saving grace, honestly. People looking from the outside, like my family, especially because they probably are my best followers on Instagram, they're always commenting about how there is a thriving Black community out here. They're just always so intrigued when I take pictures of me and my friends together. I always tell people when they move here, you have to be intentional. It won't just happen because we're all spread out. You have to go out of your way to attend events when they're posted. You can't just wait for the invite. I'm glad there were things when I moved here that opened me up, too. I had never hiked before really. I did try skiing. Oh my gosh, camping! That was never in my wheelhouse before this man and his family took me camping.

JAMES: *So the two of you built a life here. Brandon already had two kids, and now you have five, total, which is, I think, the Utah standard. People always talk about how this is such a great place to raise a family. How has it been raising a Black family here, with so little diversity?*

MICHELLE: Well, again, Mommy was intentional. I'd be at an event and see a Black woman playing the piano. I'm like, "Do you do lessons?" If I was looking for a dance center, I'd be looking on the website for a Black teacher. We don't tap dance, but let's go ahead and take tap from this Black teacher. That's how we started at the dance center. We stayed, we got to know the owner, and then we infiltrated the family. Those relationships are key.

It's not easy raising a Black family in Utah sometimes because passive aggressive things happen sometimes. I could tell we were an anomaly, right? Like, not only did other people see Black kids, but behind them were two Black parents. I had to be cautious to not make them over-conscious about it. I think that's where Love-Day Educational Consulting started. There were so many kids isolated at their schools in Utah.

How are they going to be able to stand up and know who they are? I'm giving that to my kids and my home, but how can I equip other parents who don't have the education privilege? I have to navigate this political, religious education space—they say church and state are separated, but in Utah, it's all mixed in. I'm not a business person at all, but now, for the last three years, I've run the business for that purpose.

I think it was just like when I went natural with my hair twelve years ago. After having a baby, your hair kind of looks different. I was just tired of it, and it was dry out here. I had no YouTube, I had no hairstylist, but my hair was so dry, and I just couldn't maintain it with the relaxer. So we were getting ready to go to a barbecue, and I'm like, I'm gonna go do my hair. I go to the bathroom and I look at it, and I just cut it.

So I started going through that natural hair journey. I was an administrator, I was a principal, and one mom came up to me and said, "Thank you so much for being yourself." She said, "My daughter got to see a Black woman with natural hair occupying spaces with men in suits and still being able to carry on business and not worry about it." It just hit me like, *I'm just walking in with an afro because I didn't know what to do with my hair.* I'm trying to figure it out and I'm self-conscious, and it was my husband from Wyoming who said, "You should do dreads. Who says it's not professional?"

We had this whole back and forth about the Americanized viewpoint of how hair should look. With those missteps along the way, I realized I was helping young girls whenever I'd walk into a school building. I can be with the superintendent with my hair like that. Betty Sawyer, I think, helped a lot too, because I would watch her with her dreads. Then, of course, thankfully, the natural hair movement caught up to where I was.

JAMES: *So tell us a little more about Love-Day Consulting and Rise Virtual Academy. You were at Granite School District, which was one of the most diverse, but you really wanted to make an impact. How did you make the change?*

MICHELLE: So I had started the LLC for Love-Day Educational Consulting in 2017, but I didn't know how to balance the two, my day job and consulting, so that it wouldn't overlap. The whole point was to be able to help families advocate for their children of color, especially in IEP, individualized educational plan, meetings. Then a lot of the people who would call me would end up being in the school district I worked in. So it overlapped, and it just wasn't working well. Then I started thinking out of the box and doing brown bag lunches to talk with parents and taking my lunch time.

Well, COVID helped transform so many things for the better for me. I was sitting there, just frustrated. My twelve-year-old had done a run/walk for Ahmaud Arbery, and that day everybody was doing the three-mile run. I didn't want to go down, so I said, "Well, we'll do it here in solidarity." So she and I went out to do it. I'm talking to her about why we're running and giving her a little bit of information as to why things like this happen. It was kind of the first time I talked to her about it. Then we sat down to dinner, and I got to tell her about Breanna Taylor in her bedroom. Then I started getting just sad. I think the straw on the camel's back for me was George Floyd. In a span of three weeks, I'd talked to my kids three times, just about being Black. Again, my catalyst to becoming an administrator was there was no representation, and now I'm seeing everything blow up. While everybody was just posting to social media, making their squares black, I just took a moment and started thinking I had always wanted to start a school. Friends had always been asking me when I would do it.

Brandon Day and Michelle Love-Day

That night, I just started writing everything I could do. It just was like, the kids have been virtual, and that was my inspiration.

I realized that we could teach them virtually and this is what it could look like. I started writing things down and designing Rise Academy for the safety, initially, and I brought it up to him. It literally was spawned in April, and then I started thinking, I need teachers. By June, we had teachers and the concept of students learning their Black history better than any school could teach them, beyond Dr. King and Harriet Tubman. I want them to be able to walk into a meeting and be confident that they might be the only one in that room, but they know the shoulders they stand on and the greatness they come from and will be. That's how Rise Academy started.

BRANDON: The first week, I listened in. They're talking about all the great Black inventors, all these inventors they'd never heard of. A realization came over so many of the students. One little boy said, "We invented everything." This boost of pride came over them. That was my first big realization that this is a really important thing she started here.

184

MICHELLE: Even as I was thinking about what's happening with COVID, I was also thinking about how we have to redo how we do education. Once kids learn certain concepts, they should be able to leave that grade. That's when kids get bored and disinterested. I have always thought that the grade level system is outdated, so we group them together age appropriately.

I knew that first night that we introduced this had to be big. Each grade level was named after influential Utahns, so their classes are like the Rep. Hollins classroom or the France A. Davis classroom, and they actually came on the call. The students were seeing living history right in front of them. Then our board members spoke to the kids. One of them had a crown and she goes, "I'm going to put this on my head because you all need to know that you're kings and queens." I looked on the screen and you could just see kids sitting up higher and taller.

I would go into each classroom virtually, and one of the kids was talking to Miss J, the teacher, saying she's so nice and patient, not like the other teacher. I knew what that kid was saying, because that other teacher, with our Black kids, sometimes they have their biases, and they're impatient with our kids. I've seen it first-hand. And now these kids are receiving love, even if it's virtual for now, with a Black teacher. I feel like, for me, this has to work. I feel like it's helping and saving our kids. Parents of adoptees and Black parents see it.

JAMES: *That sounds great, and you've just started your second year, so congratulations on that. Brandon, tell us a little bit about what you're working on now.*

BRANDON: I'm making commercials. After being with Brian Day and working in marketing, advertising, and building brands, I realized I really like that. For about ten years, I was out on the road, traveling as a speaker and trainer, teaching people how to invest in real estate. That was good, but it took me away from my family. As COVID-19 ended live events, I had to do a pivot. I started a digital marketing business. Over the last five months, I aligned with this company called Chamber Media. I'm the liaison between the clients and Chamber Media. We make high-end video productions for YouTube and Facebook. Most of our ads have a comedic spin. I get to be involved on the creative side and the marketing side as well. It's pretty amazing, and I like being in that space.

JAMES: *So it sounds like both of you have been intentional in a lot of ways, being there for your family and not only finding but also creating spaces for other Black families. One thing that really sticks out to me about our community is that we support one another, and you two demonstrate that.*

BRANDON: Definitely a lot of it is about showing up. That's one thing that Michelle has been really good at. I wouldn't be as social and out there if it weren't for her saying, "We're going to this event." If you're moving here and trying to connect, you have to. It really is easy to just kind of hang back and say, *They won't miss me.* You will be missed. If you don't think that a community this small needs you, you're wrong. The community needs you. I think it's about just showing up and networking. The Black Chamber events, for me, have always been great places to meet someone new because it's growing. Silicon Slopes is growing. The economy in Utah is booming right now; more and more Black people are coming into Utah, wondering where they can plug in. I would say, on the other side, reach out to invite people.

> " If you don't think that a community
> this small needs you, you're wrong.
> The community needs you. "

—BRANDON DAY

MICHELLE: That's what I had to do. I'm an ambivert, so I do thrive off of being around people. But then I need my downtime by myself to recharge. As more and more people were moving to Utah, I remembered what my first three years felt like. I wanted to be friends with them, but then I didn't have the capacity or the bandwidth to do that. I can't be friends with everybody, but I can connect them with other people.

JAMES: *I feel like our community is unique in that way, cheering each other on and trying to make those connections, which makes a difference not only for professionals but also for families with children.*

MICHELLE: It's intentional, just like supporting Black-owned businesses. When Brandon and his friend started Green Day Moving ten years ago, we saw that. To this day, I still get a few friends texting when they're about to move. They want to support Black-owned businesses, and they knew we were somewhere in the valley. I tell them that now there is a Black man who owns it with his mom, and they're still operating. Or people will ask if I know any Black people who make cakes. They just very much want to support our own. Word gets out. We help each other.

A father of two, Simbarashe accepted a job offer in Salt Lake City at Goldman Sachs in 2013. A Zimbabwe native who moved to the United States in 2005 to complete his undergraduate studies in computer science and earned a master's degree at West Chester University in Pennsylvania, Simbarashe is now a vice president and senior engineer at Goldman's Salt Lake City office. As he built his career, he also has become a voice of influence when it comes to attracting diverse talent and mentoring young people with a knack for engineering.

JAMES: *So what was going through your mind, coming from Philadelphia to Salt Lake?*

SIMBARASHE: Well, I got an offer with Goldman Sachs, so I think my first emotion was that I was very happy about that. You know, I'm a huge basketball fan. I knew about the Jazz—and I am a student of the game—so I knew a bit about Utah before I moved here from that perspective. Quite frankly, I was okay with the move. It wasn't until I started to share with friends and family, and I had those conversations, that I began questioning the decision.

I started doing Google searches, trying to find out more about the Black community. To be fair, at the time I moved, in 2013, a lot of the narrative that was out there was not very attractive for Black professionals. I was young, looking to enjoy those formative years after college. But my wife—who was then my girlfriend—and I, we took the plunge together.

We saw this as a great opportunity for us. When I moved here, I gave myself two years to see how it was, and if I didn't like it, I was going to look for the next thing. That first year was difficult.

I lived downtown at the Gateway. I didn't venture out much, outside of going to the office and coming back home. I went to a couple of football games and went to a couple of basketball games, but that was really it. Fast forward nine years, and I'm still here. I'm married, and my two daughters were born here. We own a home, and career-wise, things are going well. It's been a good ride.

JAMES: *Utah has that effect on people. Tell us a little bit about your passion for engineering.*

SIMBARASHE: I've loved engineering since I was eleven years old. When I started as an engineer at Goldman Sachs, I knew how to code, I knew how to do all these things, but I had a little bit of imposter syndrome. As a Black engineer, there's not that many of us you see out there on a day-to-day basis. It took me finding mentors and coaches to get comfortable. I want to help the kids that look like me, that otherwise would never have thought that they could make it as an engineer, as a geek, as somebody that spent time on a computer, writing code, doing all these things that might not necessarily be cool.

I've also been extremely fortunate to work for a company that believes in the same things that I'm talking about. We've done a lot within our community here in Utah, and broadly across the nation, where we're trying to figure out creative ways to teach computer science, to get kids on this journey from a very, very young age and trying to find ways to impact kids. We want them to be inspired by engineers who came to their school, who came to their communities.

JAMES: *Talk to us a little bit about your family life. You met your wife in your freshman year of college, in West Virginia. You two were dating when you moved here?*

SIMBARASHE: We were really good friends through college, and then, post-college, we started dating, and I moved to Philadelphia where I did my master's program. Then we moved to Utah together, got engaged, and got married here in downtown at the Roman Catholic Cathedral in 2015.

JAMES: *You have two daughters?*

SIMBARASHE: We've got a three-year-old and a one-year-old. My oldest daughter has started skiing. We are embracing the activities and things to do here in Utah, and they enjoy it. It's been a fantastic place for us to raise our family. Utah's safe and clean, and we've just really loved it from that perspective.

JAMES: *What about the social aspect? Do you connect with other Black families who have children? What has that experience been like for you?*

SIMBARASHE: I'm extremely lucky that my employer, from a diversity perspective, does really well in terms of attracting and retaining talent. There are a lot of young families as well, so through my work network, I know of folks that have kids who are the same age as my kids.

But the other interesting thing is the fact that Utah also has a huge Mormon population. A ton of folks will do missions out there in different parts of the world, and they bring those cultures here to Utah. I speak my own native language, sometimes when we're in the store, or out and about. If my daughter is misbehaving, and I want to tell her something, I'll use my native language. There have been a couple instances where somebody will hear me and they'll ask, "Are you from Zimbabwe?"

We've met some folks that have traveled to Zimbabwe or that part of the world and shared experiences with them. You build relationships and friendships because of that. So we've been able to find those relationships inside of our new communities, but also more broadly, with folks who have actually experienced our culture and have been to Zimbabwe and understand some of those nuances. It's been really good.

JAMES: *You've been an important part of helping to attract more professionals, too. I know mentorship is important to you, and you've worked hard to connect and create opportunities for other Black families. I also want to mention that, a few years ago, you started a chapter of the National Society of Black Engineers here. What was your motivation behind that?*

SIMBARASHE: When I started my professional career, we had these employee resource groups, and I was part of a team trying to figure out how to recruit more diverse talent to our Salt Lake City office. So we sat down with a bunch of colleagues and started figuring out where those pockets of talented engineers and talented professionals are who might not know that there are careers here in Salt Lake City. National Society of Black Engineers, NSBE, was one such organization. Goldman already participated in a ton of initiatives with NSBE.

Locally, we then started exploring, going to regional NSBE conferences. If you look at Utah, it sits in a region with some of the mountain states as well as the West Coast states. Part of the motivation there was trying to find kids that have that "locality" to this region of the country. It was interesting because we started to solve the question of how to attract, by going to NSBE, partnering up with initiatives throughout the year, going to the conventions, and mentoring. But every time I would go to either the regional or the national conventions, I would talk to a ton of people who would ask me the same question: What is it like in Utah?

Or I'd meet other professionals that interviewed with Utah companies who had maybe dropped out of the process because they were unsure about the community. Or, I'd meet people that were engineers at the conventions who were at other Utah companies right here in the valley. For me, it was like, *Well, where are these people?* We didn't have a way to connect.

Looking at those different streams of engagement, we got together with a group of people, and we decided to start a professional NSBE chapter in Salt Lake City. Our goal was to provide an opportunity for professionals to come together and create community and also to share ideas. When people come to Utah, it shouldn't just be about that one company that you're coming to. As a secondary objective, we wanted to provide mentorship to the NSBE collegiate chapters that were here in Utah. So over the years, the different universities would have a chapter, but then the president and the vice president graduate and the chapter sort of dissolves for a couple years. We wanted to provide, as a professional chapter, that mentoring and coaching, and also that continuity.

We've been doing events for the last five years, so much so that, at one of the Silicon Summit events, we were able to bring in the previous executive director for NSBE to talk, and he facilitated a discussion on diversity, inclusion, and equity. So we've built some really strong relationships with NSBE over the years. One of the goals that we have is to bring a NSBE convention to Utah, whether that's a regional one that brings two or three thousand or the national one that attracts fifteen thousand plus engineers. That's one of our goals, to have NSBE descend on Salt Lake City, showcase what's happening within Silicon Slopes and in the valley at large, and open up more opportunities for people who look like us that might not have looked at Utah as a potential place to start their careers.

JAMES: *I feel like people in our community have worked hard to connect people. We're trying to engage and collaborate. Have you experienced that?*

SIMBARASHE: You can't hide the fact that, from a demographic perspective, there are not a lot of Black folks in Utah. When people hear that, that seems like it's a bad thing, but I actually think it's a good thing. It brings people together.

When I first moved here, I would go to the grocery store or the mall and bump into other Black professionals. You know, you have the nod, people acknowledging that they see you. Through that, I started having random conversations with people in grocery stores, talking about their backgrounds, what brought them to Utah, etc. Over the years, I still get the nods, but there's a lot more people, so it's not as frequent as it used to be. Community is important, James, because the only way that I think we will attract people to Utah and get them to stay and help build awareness about all the opportunities that exist in Utah is with a strong community.

> " The only way that I think we will attract people to Utah and get them to stay and help build awareness about all the opportunities that exist in Utah is with a strong community. "

—SIMBARASHE MAPONGA

I've talked to a ton of professionals who will interview for everything from entry level to executive level jobs, love the company, love the work—but for a lot of them, they didn't see the community that exists for them, for their children, for their families, and so they chose elsewhere. Having that community, and the work that you and other people are doing as a resource to professionals who are looking to come here, is so important. They need to know that there's a community here, there are churches and places to get your hair done, ethnic food, all of the culture. Having a strong community allows us to tell that story in a meaningful, positive way to continue to attract people to come here and stay.

JAMES: *I think we are getting better at building that as we identify more people. What was it that shifted for you? What plugged you into that sense of community?*

SIMBARASHE: You know, I've always been somebody that's ambitious. With my company, I was able to get opportunities really early in my career to do things that perhaps, if I'd been in a hub location, would have taken a little bit longer to do. In my early days in Utah, I went to work and I came home, and we were miserable, to be honest with you. On weekends, we'd go to Vegas, we would go to LA, travel outside of the state. Then one of my really good friends challenged me to give Utah a try.

I started to do more "Utah things." I started going skiing and snowboarding. When I was on the East Coast, we had skiing and snowboarding, but I had never experienced that. I started doing some of that here in Utah, and I got more plugged into the community, meeting other professionals—yourself and other folks who helped plug me into a lot of things that were happening within the valley. The Black Chamber, as an example, has been a fantastic community gathering place. I've gone to Nights in Harlem, where I met other Black professionals.

Another thing that has kept me here was that I got an inter-esting opportunity to serve as a commissioner on the governor's MLK Human Rights Commission in 2018. I'm an engineer, so I didn't know what my impact would be on such a commission. But I had a lot of support, I worked with a lot of really smart people. That helped me understand how I can use my expertise to have a positive impact in the community. As part of the MLK Commission every year, when we honor and celebrate Dr. King's birthday in January, we've now, for the last two or three years running, partnered up with Goldman Sachs and the Utah Jazz. We invite kids from Title One schools to learn coding skills, with a caveat that, as part of that learning experience, those kids get to spend that day learning about the six principles of non-violence. They're learning about coding, going to a Jazz game, singing the National Anthem, and sitting behind the players. Some of those experiences, James, I never would have had in other places. That has helped bind me to the Utah community.

EIGHT

Arts, Dining, and Entertainment

When you think of Utah, you think of its great outdoors and top economy. What most don't think about is its nightlife. In 2017, during the NBA playoffs, the Golden State Warriors took a dig at Salt Lake City's nightlife saying that it "lulls you to sleep being so boring." The Utah Jazz responded with creating a #nightlife T-shirt with sale proceeds benefiting their 5FortheFight mission for cancer research.

In addition to having one of the strongest research institutions in the country, Utah does have quite the nightlife, contrary to what some NBA players believe. Just like its diversity, you just have to be aware and look for it. Bars and clubs may not be its strength. Laws force the bars to be more spread, out and liquor laws can be challenging to navigate at times. But when you think about Utah's overall culture, family-oriented, small community, and overall winning environment, it creates unbelievable talent. Utah is home to many talented musicians, bands and vocalists who perform nationally and globally, have appeared on the popular shows — *America's Got Talent,*

The Voice, and *American Idol*—won Grammy awards, and produced platinum albums.

In 2011, the Utah Black Chamber hosted its very first event. Black businesses in Utah were, and still are at times, difficult to find, so we wanted to create an event that draws them out. What better way than food and music? We hired a band, brought in hamburgers and hot dogs. Most of the people who attended were my church family and friends, but over time we began discovering the businesses we wanted to help and establishing the connections we needed to make in order to provide them with the necessary resources. This event was simple, yet people had a great time and looked forward to the next one. So, the community BBQ remained as an annual event, and we continued to build on it. We added activities for everyone and their kids, gave away prizes and brought in better food. In a few years, we began to bring in BBQ from one of our local members. The event continued to grow, gained more exposure, and in 2016, we partnered with another organization to deepen the impact of bringing people together to identify diverse businesses, and this event gave an opportunity to bring people together, build bridges, create connections, and elevate Utah's diversity.

Excellence in the community showcases local talent, hosting nearly one hundred free concerts all throughout Utah. Its main concert series is held in downtown Salt Lake City at the Gallivan Center. One of the most popular bands, Changing Lanes Band, performs a Motown Show that draws one of its largest crowds. In collaboration with Excellence and Changing Lanes, the Black Chamber invited caterers and food trucks and activities for the kids, and in three years, the crowd grew from a few hundred to nearly eight thousand people of all different backgrounds dancing, singing, and witnessing an experience not commonly seen in Utah. What began as a small community event to discover small businesses now brings a larger purpose.

The Gallivan Center is one of many concert and event venues. Small and large, indoor and outdoor, Utah has attractive event spaces that have brought talent from all over and from different genres all year long. What's great about many of these venues is community accessibility. Utah is strong in its local events, and the community loves to support each other.

Utah provides many opportunities for talented artists to thrive. In addition to Park City hosting the popular Sundance Film Festival, Cedar City hosts the Shakespeare Festival. There are several other theater, film, and acting companies, and many popular movies have been filmed in Utah, including *Sandlot, Thelma and Louise, High School Musical, Transformers*, and *Independence Day*. I was even privileged to be an extra in a couple of TV shows filmed locally. You'll also find museums, art galleries, and community and innovation centers providing space and opportunity for up-and-coming creatives to hone their craft.

An event the chamber felt was missing in the Black community was a formal gala. An opportunity for the community to socialize at an event where people put on their best outfits. So, chamber leadership came together to discuss a networking event during Black History Month, and Evening in Harlem was conceived. The Harlem Renaissance is the artistic explosion for Black Americans, and that time period is a favorite theme for event attire at New Year's Eve parties and other events. The chamber felt this sort of event would be a great opportunity to showcase the various creative talent from the Black community in another event to strengthen the connection in Utah's BIPOC community. Live music, spoken word, art, and activities such as dancing and a casino attracts people from all of Utah and beyond. What most people don't know is that Utah has a connection to the Harlem Renaissance. Wallace Thurman was an American novelist who also wrote essays and was a publisher of newspapers and literary journals. He was best known for his novel *The Blacker the Berry*, which explores discrimination within the Black community based on skin color, with lighter skin being more highly valued. Thurman was born in Salt Lake City and was a member of Calvary Baptist Church before moving to New York to become a part of the Harlem Renaissance.

While Utah doesn't have a signature dish like a Chicago dog or a New York pizza, you'll find our love for Ranch dressing and fry sauce. Several of our local restaurants have been featured in the popular show *Diners, Drive-ins and Dives*. Growing up, though, Black-owned restaurants rarely existed. We were lucky to have a soul food restaurant here and there that stayed open for a couple of years at a time, but now you'll find restaurants, food trucks, and even a brewery from northern to southern Utah. You'll find different kinds of cuisines from soul food, African, and Caribbean. The Black community in Utah is not a monolith, which makes the community even more vibrant, creative, and innovative. Many cultures are represented here, and what better way to experience a culture than through their food? And as the Black community continues to thrive, we look forward to experiencing many more restaurants opening here in Utah.

Award-winning ballerina Katlyn Addison is the first black Principal Ballerina for Ballet West in Salt Lake City. Born in Ontario, Canada, Katlyn started her training at the age of ten with the National Ballet School of Canada and continued her training with Quinte Ballet, Houston Ballet II, Pacific Northwest Ballet, Boston Ballet, and Houston Ballet Ben Stevenson Academy. She has danced at Ballet West since 2011.

JAMES: *So what was it that prompted you to move to Utah?*

KAT: I came to Utah because of Ballet West. That's what brought me here, but I have fallen in love with the city and the mountains.

JAMES: *Share a little bit about your background.*

KAT: I'm Canadian-Caribbean. My mom is from Trinidad and Tobago, and my dad is from Windsor, England, and Jamaica. They migrated to Canada—Toronto on the East Coast—when they were young.

JAMES: *So when did you arrive in the States?*

KAT: About seventeen years ago. I moved from Canada to the Houston Ballet and was there for seven years before I moved to Utah. My whole time in the States I have been dancing as a classical ballerina. It's kind of weird to say, but my first job and my job to do this day is classical ballet. That's what brought me to this space.

JAMES: *How did you become passionate about dance?*

KAT: It started with me dancing around in my parents' room. I was fortunate from the start. When I was growing up, both of my parents were working, and they told me, my brother, and my sister that we could accomplish anything we wanted. And I wanted to dance. My family and I would go watch the National Ballet of Canada perform, and I dreamt of being on the stage, wearing the crown and tutu. I had the opportunity to study at good ballet schools—the National Ballet School of Canada, Houston Ballet, Boston Ballet, and Pacific Northwest Ballet; they are all very prestigious names. I also did piano competitions and played the

Images courtesy of Ballet West

flute in a band, which helped my musicality as a dancer. I'm still living out my dream. I feel very fortunate that I get to do what I love to do every day.

And now I see my niece dance around the house, like I did as a child. She has her own little flow — she's just like a butterfly. I'm like, *Oh, that reminds me of myself.* That's what got me into it. I saw it on stage. I aspired to be that ballerina.

JAMES: *So what's a day in the life of a ballerina like?*

KAT: It's unique. I wake up and I'm at the studios from nine to seven, Monday through Friday, and then I usually teach on weekends. I don't really have a lot of time to play. I wake up, I go to class, we rehearse ballets that are upcoming, and I do it Monday through Friday. We do five different performance runs each season, and our season runs from August to June.

JAMES: *Does it take a toll going from 9:00 a.m. to 7:00 p.m.?*

KAT: It's hard. I am very thankful that we have the mountains right here. Hiking actually helps my stamina. It also helps me stay in shape when I'm not dancing. When I have my offseason, which is usually June and July, I have opportunities to rejuvenate and recover. Anytime I have a break, I'll try to get away, but it doesn't always work.

For example, I was recently commissioned to choreograph a new work for Kansas City Ballet. I spent my week off this last fall working with their company, and the piece will be premiered in March of 2022. It was an amazing opportunity, because I am working towards becoming a choreographer when I transition away from professional dance. Sometimes I get stressed from balancing my dancing career while also trying to develop my voice as a choreographer, but I find ways to rejuvenate by traveling or by going to the mountains or by being around good people. I also love to cook.

JAMES: *It is nice to have mountains that are so accessible. You have the chance to experience nature. It's almost like a natural gym, too.*

KAT: Exactly. It's also spiritual; that peace and quiet is so beautiful. With ballet, even though we're not talking, I'm constantly thinking about how we tell a story without words. I'm constantly imagining a narrative of how I'm expressing myself. When I get up into the mountains and experience silence again, I feel like it's a spiritual experience for me, so it not only helps with my stamina, but it's also where I can find my center again—balance and peace.

JAMES: *It's just incredible to have the kind of access we do—bike ride or trails or public transit—to see the world from eight thousand feet above. I love that aspect and the peace you're talking about. Thinking about the entertainment society—artists, creatives—what attracted you to Salt Lake City and Ballet West? How did they recruit you here from Houston?*

KAT: Well, when I first moved to Utah, I did not know what to expect. I just assumed there would not be a lot of diversity, and compared to other places I have lived, there really wasn't as much. Slowly but surely, though, people are migrating here. I had very low expectations of Utah, even though I know a lot of people move here for the mountains, like we've talked about, and now I see it as a tucked away secret. I think it's a really great place for young entrepreneurs; there's space for us—meaning every race—to grow and start something of our own. I do feel like Utah's a great place for that. And there's lots of opportunities.

" I think it's a really great place for young entrepreneurs; there's space for us—meaning every race—to grow and start something of our own. "

—KAT ADDISON

Regarding what brought me here, years ago, I competed at a Youth America Grand Prix competition; it's a ballet competition. It was the first time they held a job fair, and it was basically a ballet studio. You're in a big cube in a studio with a panel of ballet artistic directors. There were thousands of us in the studio, and they had to make cuts every two exercises. After the second exercise, Adam Sklute the artistic director at Ballet West, offered me a job. When I was talking to Adam, he said he'd been watching my career over the years, and I do remember seeing him when I was at Houston Ballet. At the time, I wanted the change. I got the job within two exercises.

JAMES: *That's amazing. Can you tell us what the industry is like in terms of diversity?*

KAT: When people picture a jewelry box ballerina, they're usually picturing a Caucasian ballerina. The values are changing, though. Over the past two years or so, and even with COVID, I feel like it has created more awareness, especially in the classical ballet world. There are a lot of really talented, really technically trained classical ballerinas of color out there. Given the right opportunity, they will flourish. I mean, I was just promoted to Principal Dancer at Ballet West. I have been—excuse my language—dancing my butt off. I've been dancing like crazy. It was, in due time, right for this opportunity to come for me. There are another two Black ballerinas who just got promoted at the National Ballet of Canada. I feel that artistic directors are realizing that they have had a biased lens, and their perspective is shifting. I feel like Adam Sklute has been a great boss. So many opportunities have come for me in my career as a performer being at Ballet West. I've been here for ten years, and every other year, I get promoted. Any time we go on tour, Adam has made sure I'm doing a featured role as well. I've earned it. I've worked hard for it, but he is also unafraid to amplify my talent even though other directors haven't done that with dancers of color.

Also, our audience, meaning the people who are coming to the ballet, is changing. I feel like there are a lot of people like us who are going to the ballet or stepping into that atmosphere, which helps as well. It's the people who love it, the people that come and buy tickets for the performance, they are going to help my career. If I have a following and a fan base, it will help me continue to rise to the highest rankings as a classical ballerina.

Playing music since he was a kid at church, CJ Drisdom has helped catalyze the music scene in Utah. He's a musician, and founder of BL4CK Utah, a new nonprofit that aims to educate, inspire, and rally Black men. He's also the founder of the group Changing Lanes, a party rock funk soul show band that made it all the way to *America's Got Talent*.

James: *Let's start with national television. What was that like?*

CJ: What a phenomenal opportunity to meet so many different talented people from around the world. Yeah, we made it to the top 11, which was really cool. We got to meet everybody who was there, who made it through to that level, so we now have several relationships all over the world. I still talk to the horn players, all of the dancers, trapeze artists, and all these people I met. These are people you know are going to do a good job with life, and they're not going to stop.

JAMES: *So exciting, and you just keep moving up. Speaking of which, what do you think caused the shift from Utah being behind the times to now being this hidden gem, like we're next up?*

CJ: A lot of it is people genuinely caring about their craft. For yourself, being the chamber president, you're going to do what you can to make sure people have resources. You're taking personal responsibility outside of your job.

So, with music, I worked at one of my jobs for eight hours and gave them their time, sometimes a little bit of overtime. I would literally match those hours when I got home with music. So I'll come home, and go downstairs and be working on my music for eight hours, because I didn't believe in giving time to that and then not giving time to me and my music and the people that are going to eventually be following me. I was just doing what I could do to be the very best that I could be for myself. I'm working to build a community, and that's how this thing shifted, right? It's really in the community. Let's figure this thing out, and let's move this thing along. So let's do the music for the chamber and let's push that along, and that's what everybody in Utah is kind of figuring out now: *Oh, I can do this, or I can be an artist, or I can be an account manager.* Not everybody's going to be the leader, but they can lead at their level.

JAMES: *I love that. Shifting for a moment, let's talk about Kanye West's Sunday Service and how that came together in just a few days.*

CJ: So they called me on a Wednesday and said they were in need of somebody. *Also, you can't say nothing, but Kanye West is coming here, and we want to facilitate this thing and get everything done.* In the end, they reached out to the tourism family. That's what they said, right? So he handed me the number to the producers. I said, "Okay, when do they come in?" And the answer was "tomorrow." I started thinking about my schedule. I had a wedding at the Grand America on Friday, and I knew that was going to take all day because I'm playing it. Then I had a wedding on Saturday in Jackson Hole that we were going to travel to right after the one on Friday. So I had to find a bass player for my band to go to Jackson Hole with. I did that, and they were all jealous because they wanted to stay and be part of this situation. So it's Thursday when they pick those guys up from the Sheraton downtown, and

*CJ hosting Kanye West's Sunday Service at
the Gateway Downtown Salt Lake City*

then it was three guys in the car with me, the two producers and the stage guy, and we literally went searching for venues. I call about security. We get in touch with the fire chief, all of that stuff, and get the permit the same day. Everything we needed from the city and the state of Utah came through, and I want to thank former Mayor Jackie Biskupski for that. She dug in.

At the end of the day, it was between the Capitol and the Gateway Mall, and the Capitol had a wedding that day, but they were willing to pay to get that wedding out. I said, "Let's leave it there." I called the Gateway and said, "Y'all need to take this." We had thirty-five thousand people there that afternoon. It was the largest conference they've ever had there.

And then we had twenty-five thousand people there when Changing Lanes was there on July 4th. Every restaurant was overcapacity. The only thing we didn't have that Kanye had was people hanging off buildings.

JAMES: *It was called a Sunday Service. It was a Sunday gospel choir, right?*

CJ: It was.

JAMES: *Wow. They called right out of the blue and found you and a community that was just going to make it happen. And your brother Tim Drisdom has something with the Salt Lake City Mass Choir, right?*

CJ: Yes, the record was released and got a number one gospel EP in the world; it won an Emmy Award. That was a huge accomplishment. I got to meet all these people: Kirk Franklin, PJ Morton, Yolanda Adams. I mean we were in Vegas for stellar awards, and it was amazing. Now we're working with several artists. We're just grateful for all these opportunities and the blessing God has bestowed on us because of our faithfulness, because of our consistency, because of our integrity and the respect we have for people. We're trying to be a blessing to the people around us.

JAMES: *All of that success helps validate that Utah is a hidden gem, bringing those type of gospel influencers.*

CJ: That has never happened before. We literally brought the first gospel situation, major artists, here to Utah. We're grateful for that, and they want to come back, so we're trying to cultivate this community and continue bringing gospel artists here on a regular basis. They want to be here, and they're telling their friends. If we make it a regular thing, Utah can be another hub for gospel music.

JAMES: *And that will spill over from the evangelical community into the secular community; right?*

CJ: That's right, and we have so much more work to do. As long as we keep teaming up and bringing in people who maybe have a different mindset or who are maybe smarter than you or me, we're making progress. I surround myself with people who are just better than me, always. You can't be in the room with me if you're not better than me at something. I want to learn. I want to be better. We hurt ourselves by not allowing people around us who are better than us.

JAMES: *The idea is to bring folks together to help all of us rise up, to not have this constant competition happening.*

CJ: Oftentimes, I tell people now, I'm not competing against you, and because I'm not competing against you, I'm competing against myself. There's a better me to be had. If we just concentrate on ourselves, that makes us better individuals. Then you can bring that to the table.

JAMES: *That's a great perspective in terms of personal development. To look back a little bit, I know your family has always been musically inclined. Was it your dad who inspired you to get into music?*

CJ: My dad and my mom. My dad plays keys; my mom would sing in the choir and my dad was directing it at Holy Pilgrim Church of God in Christ. My pastor, Gabriel Jackson Sr., allowed me and my brother and cousin to play drums in the church, when we were like five or six. So we started with drums, playing for the choir. Ryan Smalls was the main drummer, and we learned from him as he was playing. He would let us play songs that were in between stuff, and then all of a sudden, we started playing all the choir songs. Then my brother Tim began to play organ at eleven years old. My parents bought me a keyboard, and I couldn't learn fast enough. I'd sit there and learn a song, and then we'd go in there and play it without even practicing it. Then I told my parents I want a bass, and my mom was dating this guy named Shannon. He gave me a bass guitar, brand new, that he'd never played. At seventeen, I started playing bass, and it came really easy for me. You know, some of it I learned on my grandmother's couch. We all lived in a one-bedroom in my grandmother's house, bunk beds for six years. My family has been through quite a bit, and I'm grateful for that. You know, when I busted the window because I was mad, everybody was cold that night. We learned a lot, and we grew together as a family. I don't think there's a family as close as we are, honestly. We did all that. I was seventeen playing the bass, my brother was playing the organ, and my cousin was playing the drums—and we just went for it, man.

" I was seventeen playing the bass, my brother was playing the organ, and my cousin was playing the drums—and we just went for it, man. "

—CJ DRISDOM

LIZ LAMBSON

An artist, musician, writer, and mother to five boys, Liz Lambson performs as a string bassist with the Ballet West Orchestra and is the creator of "Yoga Storytime & Songs," where she performs as the beloved children's singer-songwriter Lizzy Luna. She also serves as a board member of the Utah Black Artist Collective and is the Executive Director of the new Utah Black History Museum. In the summer of 2020, she was one of a team of artists who painted a Black Lives Matter mural in front of Salt Lake City's city hall.

JAMES: *So, your name is connected to so many different aspects of our community: music, art, museums. You were even recently commissioned to create murals around Salt Lake City. How did Utah attract Liz Lambson?*

LIZ: The simple answer is that my husband got a job here. If I get a little deeper into it, we moved her from Kansas City, Missouri, four years ago, and I loved it there. It's the first place I've lived where there was a substantial Black community. I grew up in Colorado Springs. My dad's Black, my mom's Korean, and we were raised in a very white neighborhood. After marrying my husband, we lived in Portland, Oregon, we lived in upstate New York, we lived in Orange County, and we lived in Kansas City. We settled there, and I just loved it. I loved walking around and not feeling different. Anyway, a job opportunity came up for him here in Salt Lake. I really was resistant initially. What attracted me, though, is that we have friends here, we knew people here. Specifically, I knew there were opportunities here for me. I knew there was a strong music and arts community here and that I would be able to find a place. And that has proven to be true.

" I knew there was a strong music and arts community here and that I would be able to find a place. And that has proven to be true. "

−LIZ LAMBSON

JAMES: *A lot of people don't think about an arts and music community existing in Utah. Why do you think that's the case?*

LIZ: People are drawn to Utah because of its reputation for the great outdoors: mountain climbing, rock climbing, skiing, hiking, camping, and the rock formations in southern Utah—all of these outdoor things. Those are the very in-your-face characteristics of Utah, so you find people moving here from all over the country who are very passionate about those kinds of outdoor sports or just that adventurous lifestyle. I do think it's sort of under the radar or just not as well known that Utah has a really strong and vibrant arts community. Just the way you'll see real excellence and professionalism in the sports community in athletics, you will also see a really high level of skill, performance, and talent in the arts. When I say arts, I mean like music, dance, drama, comedy, writing—all forms.

I've also noticed a really special community dynamic here, where people want to be the best at what they do and then they inspire each other. It's not about bringing each other down, right? It's about elevating us all to a higher level of performance in whatever we do. So I love that there is so much collaboration that happens here.

For example, in the orchestra scene, you can play gigs down in Provo or in Salt Lake and you end up gigging with the same people, so you get to know everybody. It's like a family.

JAMES: *Wonderful, and I agree. Tell us a little bit about your story. How long have you been playing the string bass?*

LIZ: It's always been a huge part of my life, but I was in third grade when I had a teacher who was really, really passionate about art. She introduced me to all the classical artists, and Picasso, Da Vinci, Monet, Mondrian. Then the same year there was a little string program that opened up for the elementary school. I started that and, at the same time, I really started getting into art. Both of those things happened together. I began training and developing those skills just in parallel, as I grew, and then I decided to study music in college. I have a music degree, but I still do art. Then I'm also really passionate about writing, so I do have an English minor and I write as well. I classify myself as a creative.

My husband's a businessman; he went to the Cornell Business School, and I think that being attached to him I've learned a lot about business and running organizations. And I think that's part of what's led me to the position that I'm in now as executive director of the Utah Black History Museum. I was brought on to the project "Paint The Bus." Then I was like, okay, what's next? And there wasn't a clear plan of how to get from that point—from an empty, gutted, but beautifully painted bus—to the launch of a mobile museum. You know, there were a lot of things that needed to happen between point A and point B. So that's when I was like, *I painted this bus, and I will not let it sit here. I will not let it fail.*

When I put my name on things, I'm going to make it happen. So I was really driven from that point to do whatever we needed to do to get to a functional museum. So a big part of that was just starting the nonprofit, and we were approved earlier this year.

In the meantime, Lex is super busy with her other forms of activism. The museum—this traveling bus museum—was her idea. She didn't have all the time to invest towards it, so we pulled in Taryn Mitchell, the historian, and I started working with Taryn trying to put everything together. It took a lot of work, but we pulled it all together: artifacts, informational displays, and more. There's still a lot to do, finishing details. Then of course, the museum is always changing and growing. We want to mix it up and not always show the same things. Anyway, we launched in February for Black History Month, and it's been really successful. There's a really high demand for it. We did a ton of festivals and community events in the summertime.

JAMES: *It seems like your understanding of the business side of things—now coupled with nonprofit functions—would be a benefit to you as a creative.*

LIZ: Yes, you have to build a name for yourself. For me, that started with that first mural and then from there, I was invited to do more. What's really cool about painting murals is they will be seen. There are so many artists and they spend, you know, thousands of hours doing their amazing art, and then maybe they'll submit to a gallery show competition, and maybe it'll be rejected or maybe it'll get in and it'll be up in a gallery. I'm thinking specifically about, say, the Springville Art Museum Spring Salon; they accept art submissions from around the whole state. You can go and see some of the best visual art from the most amazing artists in the state—but these pieces are only up for a short period of time. For me, I've been fortunate enough to have a unique personal perspective that people are interested in, and that's where we get back to Black Lives Matter. Utah is a majority white state, but you have the white population of Utah suddenly wanting to learn more about the Black experience. I found people turning to me, looking for visual representations of the Black experience through art.

A professional singer-songwriter from the age of fifteen, Bri Ray was born and raised in Utah. She blends influences of R&B, soul, and pop to express her own unique voice. She's performed across the nation and also been honored as the first-ever Presidential Scholar of the Arts in singer-songwriting.

JAMES: *So, what got you into singing and songwriting? Usually, it's people's background in church, but I don't want to assume it's the same for everybody.*

BRI RAY: Actually, it was not church. I was raised LDS, and anyone familiar with their culture knows the music is not poppin'. My mom was very strict. I actually wasn't allowed to listen to any music outside of LDS music and, like, Disney Channel pop stars. My exposure to music was very limited. I was also a very shy kid, and the gospel songs my dad shared with me helped me love music. That's when I started singing and understanding that I actually had a good voice and enjoyed it. It became an easy way for me to put feelings into words and to express myself at a young age. I just fell in love with it and never stopped.

" It became an easy way for me to put feelings into words and to express myself at a young age. I just fell in love with it and never stopped. "

—BRI RAY

JAMES: *That's beautiful. So tell us where you've been so far.*

BRI RAY: I did a lot locally from about fifteen to nineteen. I did a lot of public speaking combined with music. I did *There's a Place for Everyone*, a motivational speech I would give at schools all over. So I was in Arizona and Texas and California and tons of schools in Utah, talking about kindness and acceptance and differences. So that took me all over. Then I also was a Young Arts finalist. For all the elite art schools and art high schools, the Young Arts Program is the goal to be accepted into. We found it because it was the only singer-songwriter scholarship we could find. I submitted and got accepted, so they flew me out to Miami for a week of training and networking with incredible industry professionals and all these people. They also submitted me to be a Presidential Scholar of the Arts, which I was accepted for. That took me to DC to perform at the Kennedy Center as one of the twenty Presidential Scholars of the Arts.

JAMES: *Wow. How long ago was that?*

BRI RAY: That was 2015 and 2016. I also did *American Idol* in 2015.

JAMES: *I'm finding out that we have had a lot of Utahns on* American Idol. *What about Utah County is bringing out the talent?*

BRI RAY: Utah has a super interesting music scene. Something that I'm personally passionate about working on is combining the scenes in Salt Lake and the scene in Utah County. Right now, we don't really merge very much. There's so much unique talent and different talent in both areas that once we can figure out how to bring everybody together, Utah's going to be a great place for music. Utah County is very close. The musicians all kind of know each other, and everyone's just happy to help and ready to work

Bri at one of Utah's beautiful canyons

together. There are lots of big co-writing sessions and co-writing retreats and group music nights where we test out some of our new songs that we wrote. It's a super supportive network down here.

JAMES: *That's great. It does seem like people here are looking to help and uplift each other. Are you doing music full-time then?*

BRI RAY: So I do a few things. Obviously, I do music. Then I work at a venture services firm in Provo called RevRoad. I'm the digital marketing director there. Essentially, they work like an accelerator or a venture capital firm, but instead of exchanging equity with entrepreneurs for capital directly, we exchange equity for services. So we invest services and human capital, get them set up with what they need, like a marketing team and a video team and a capital team to help them raise capital. Right now, we have around forty-two companies in our portfolio.

JAMES: *That has to keep you busy. Has marketing always been your jam?*

BRI RAY: No, actually, I was doing music full-time and being an influencer on social media, doing influencer marketing. Darrin Hill from RevRoad attended one of my Christmas concerts, heard me singing, and enjoyed my personality. He called me a week or two later and offered me the job. He had done his own research and saw what I had done with my music career as far as marketing and press and PR. So he called and asked what I had built and helped with. At that point, I had pretty much done it all on my own, so he said, "Do you think you can do it for entrepreneurs?"

JAMES: *That's great. So did you enjoy doing music full-time? What inspired you to jump into this marketing career?*

BRI RAY: I've always known that music was going to be part of my career, whether it's my main source of income or a side source. I'm still exploring that, but the opportunity to work at RevRoad allowed me to develop an entirely different section of my career and myself as an individual. At twenty-two, I was like, *This is perfect.* I have plenty of time to really decide what I want to do, and this is a great opportunity to dive in and see how I fit here.

Executive chef and owner of Sauce Boss Southern Kitchen, Julius started with a pasta food truck—a mobile restaurant and catering service in and around Salt Lake City. He's since added a popular full-service restaurant. His first foray into food service was as a catering chef at the Utah State Capitol. Then he moved into head chef positions at area restaurants before launching his entrepreneurial ventures.

James: *We're so happy to see you enjoying the kind of success you've experienced. Tell us a little bit about your background. I thought you were a native Utahn, but you spent time in Chicago as well.*

JULIUS: I was born in Chicago in the Jane Addams projects. I came here first when I was five years old, stayed three or four years, and then went back to Chicago. Every three or four years, I was moving back and forth between Utah and Chicago. It was definitely hard. Especially as a little kid, building friendships and all that stuff. My grandmother raised ten kids by herself, a single mom in the projects. She had five boys and five girls, and unfortunately, three out of the five women were addicted to crack cocaine and got caught up in the eighties and what happened there. Then me, my brother, sisters, and cousins were all victims of it as well. Moving back and forth would pertain to when my mother would get put in prison with drug charges and we had to find relatives to live with. I ended up in foster care, homeless shelters, sleeping on the street. For me, it was a scene that helped me realize I didn't want that for myself in the future.

JAMES: *Wow. Well, we're all fortunate that you were able to stay clean. So what brought Salt Lake into the picture from Chicago?*

JULIUS: Well, my grandmother wanted somewhere more slow-paced, a little more relaxing, and her son was already out here in school. He told her to come on out, that Utah is a nice, quiet, slow-paced place. And she did. I remember her bringing up the lack of diversity and how different it is in Chicago. We all kind of followed her over the decades. It was around high school when I came back again. I'd gone to my first couple years of high school in Chicago, staying in a hotel, but from then on I decided that I would stay in Utah, in Ogden. High school was the only stability I had, and I did my best in school so I could get that positive reinforcement from adults. After I graduated, I got a little job bagging groceries. That was my first bit of stability.

JAMES: *Did you find, coming to Salt Lake, any additional challenges being in a state with a lack of diversity?*

JULIUS: A lot when I was younger, when I was in second grade or sixth grade. Second grade was the first time kids asked if they could touch my hair. Or kids would ask me to hang out after school but then say their mom said they couldn't play with me. But Utah is a great state. I'm never going to deny that. Culturally, it's kind of a bubble, but it has gotten better. The biggest hurdle is that you don't have that in Chicago. Everybody looks the same; it's the white kids who look different and are the minority. Here, it was a total 180. A lot of that I discovered at a very young age, and it really puzzled me. In my opinion, it's ignorance. At the time, the only knowledge of Black people was from music, TV, and movies where we were never portrayed as the best and brightest. People were programmed from a young age to think a Black man is not as smart and is more dangerous or more aggressive. It's just the exposure to that.

JAMES: *So you've faced all those challenges to get where you are today. Tell us what got you into cooking and how you built up all that hustle, now owning Sauce Boss.*

JULIUS: Well, growing up in my grandmother's house, she'd always have leftovers in the fridge. Part of that is because she had ten kids, so she was used to cooking a lot, but another part is that she knew kids would come by hungry. So she always cooked for a lot of people, even though it was just her living there. Her food was always so good. You can taste the love she put into it. She made it to help others, and you could taste that. She knew the joy it would bring to me, somebody who maybe had lunch at school and nothing else. Going over there and tasting the food, the happiness that brought me made me think that one day I want to make others happy with my food.

" Going over there and tasting the food, the happiness that brought me made me think that one day I want to make others happy with my food. "

—JULIUS THOMPSON

JAMES: *That's an incredible story. Did you always have a restaurant in mind? You went from catering to a food truck to a restaurant, right?*

Julius Thompson, Owner of Sauce Boss Southern Kitchen

JULIUS: So, honestly, I wanted to be a pharmacist because drugs are such a big part of my life. I wanted to flip it and do something good with it. I started to work on my bachelor of science, which is required to get into pharmacy school, when I realized that I'm only doing this for the money. I was doing it for the fear of being broke again. Everybody in my family cooks, and there are great cooks in my family. I thought about my family and my family's history. I decided to call our school and change to culinary school. Like I did at other schools, I wanted recognition; I wanted praise. So I was able to do my associate's in culinary arts, and I got a 4.0, top of my class, beat out everybody. After that I worked at different kitchens, and then I got the food truck. I did that for three years. As I was looking into a restaurant, I realized that there were a lot of places doing pasta, so I was doing pasta. I thought about how I've been here all this time, and there's not a lot of food represented, you know, for Black people. There are a lot of people here now, but there's not a lot of food that represents that culture. I decided to represent my family, my grandmother, and the culture. So I did Sauce Boss Southern Kitchen.

JAMES: *It's interesting, because I remember you doing a lot of pasta in the food truck before you moved into Sauce Boss. For me, growing up, it seemed like Black restaurants just didn't last. It could have been a lack of leadership or funds, but they didn't stick around. What gives you the stability to keep your restaurant moving and growing?*

JULIUS: I think I had to do it. You've got to know your demographics as a business owner. We couldn't go in there and just do ham hocks. I love fried gizzards, but we have to look at what the demographic wants. They want stuff they know about like fried chicken, pork chops, shrimp and grits. So I've also had to educate a lot of my customers on this kind of food and the history of this kind of food. It's called Southern Kitchen, so I do sell food, too. Southern Kitchen is a more welcoming name, but the downside of that is I have people in from the South and they ask where I'm from. When I say I was born in Chicago, they wonder how I know Southern food. If you really want to go down that road, Southern food is basically slave food cooked in a big house. When slaves were freed, they had nothing to pass on but that kind of food. Soul food is just food to me. It's from our ancestors in slavery to descendants down and down and down, and we all know wherever you live in the country, this kind of food is ours.

JAMES: *How did you manage that whole process in an environment that doesn't have a lot of knowledge about soul food?*

JULIUS: You know, people are a little skittish of food if it's too foreign. I tried to put love in everything, like my grandmother did, and people can taste the love and hard work you put in the food. My biggest complaint was too much flavor, which is hilarious because a lot of people like bland food. I believe food should be made to fill you up and nourish you, and I want to give people that good food they grew up on and have them leave happy. I think that, plus educating people on what it is and what it represents, helps as well. The reason I did the food truck first is so people would know my name, building my branding and things like that. It also helped to start small and get big because people remember me from the food truck and recognize my style: big flavors, my sauce, and big portions. That's kind of my niche.

I also think that over the last few years, Utah is starting to understand more. Especially with the media, they're starting to be more exposed to Black culture and the plights of it, the culture of it, the celebrations of it. Everybody is, one way or another, recognizing and appreciating the Black experience in America.

NINE

Religious Leadership

The most important and popular questions people and families considering a move into Utah ask are, "Where can I get my hair done," "Where are the barbershops," "Where should I move for my kids to attend school," and "Would I find a church home?"

In Utah, the Black churches have always been the foundation of the Black community. Besides being a place of worship, churches have been a hub to support the community, being an advocate and community hub and voice. Churches host community events such as health and career fairs, events for the youth, and it is a space to advocate for change. Pastors are strong leaders in the Black community leading an organization considered a main hub and connector.

To connect to the Black community, you would go to church. Growing up, it's the only place where I saw my community gather in masses. The Black community seemed like such a monolith. I thought all Black people were Black and all white people were LDS. My home church, Calvary Baptist Church, was established in 1892, four years prior to Utah becoming a state. Calvary has maintained itself as a pillar of the Black community and has the largest membership of all the Black Baptist churches in Utah. Many of Utah's Black influencers are members of Calvary and on any given Sunday, local, state, and US government officials attend, police chiefs, and even celebrities are found seated in the congregation during worship services.

Calvary is a great example of the African Proverb, It takes a village to raise a child. Being a member of Calvary Baptist Church, I was blessed to be surrounded by political officials, judges, educators, and business owners. For me, growing up in a state with a small Black population, church was my extended family and place of comfort and safety. I am always my full self, being able to express "blackness" without any judgment or insecurity. I sought mentors and advice, and it was my church that not only helped me get into college but also provided the resources and scholarship opportunities so I never had to pay for college.

Believe it or not, there are more than a half dozen Black Baptist churches. These churches communicate often and support each other, attending celebration and anniversary services, and all are part of the National Baptist Convention and the Western Regional Laymen Workshop. We also have non-denominational, Pentecostal and African Methodist Episcopal (AME) churches. Trinity AME Church is the oldest Black church in Utah, established in the late 1880s. The church still worships in the same building that was erected in the early 1900s and is now marked as a Utah Historical site. In addition to the Black churches, many Black Utahns are also Catholic, Protestant, and members of non-Christian churches. The Church of Jesus Christ of Ladder Day Saints has many Black members as well.

Not everyone here is a member of the LDS Church. Utah has a church home for you no matter your religious belief, and as Utah continues to grow, the dominance of the LDS religion is becoming less.

REV. DR. FRANCE DAVIS,
PASTOR EMERITUS

Pastor Emeritus of Calvary Baptist Church in Salt Lake City, Rev. France A. Davis served his congregation as pastor for over forty-five years. Still active and still serving, he's been an influencer for his faith, for Civil Rights work in Utah, and for the Black community in general.

JAMES: *Talk to us about what you have been doing in retirement.*

REV. DAVIS: Well, I came to Utah in 1972 and worked hard, both as a professor and as a pastor of a church and other things, but then decided that it was time to change the seasons and to retire on December 31, 2019. I stepped aside and had intentions of doing an event once a month, somewhere in the world, but all of that was canceled due to COVID-19, so I've really been at home, nursing myself, dealing with sickness, and resting.

JAMES: *Are you planning to get out more now? What's next?*

REV. DAVIS: I am getting out more. In fact, my wife and I just returned from a three-week trip to Nevada and California, and we plan to be up more and more. Next month I'm going to Boise, and the month after that, I'm going to travel around the state of Utah. So I intend to go about and see some of what other people come to Utah to see. Mostly I want to see the different parks. I've been to Yellowstone, but I want to go there again. I want to go down to Zions, I want to go to the different parks and see what it is that attracts people and causes them excitement, and I want to do a lot of fishing as well.

JAMES: *So what are some of the things you miss most now that you're retired?*

REV. DAVIS: The interaction with young people; that's probably the one thing that I've missed the most, both at the church and the university where young people were students who didn't even know much of the history of Martin Luther King and Malcolm X. And then I missed the interactions at the church, with young people and with seniors. I still have some regular interaction with seniors. For example, yesterday, I visited JC Wilson, who died last night, by the way. He was an older man who I had befriended, and he had befriended me. And so I miss those two: the elderly and the young people.

JAMES: *I know you were going from about 4:00 a.m. to 11:00 p.m. every day for fifteen years. I can't even do that right now. What kept you moving like that?*

REV. DAVIS: Well, what kept me moving was God. I have that belief that God had called me to do the work that I was doing, to interact with people, to help people, to make life more meaningful for them. And that was God's business. So my role was to cast the vision, and the role of the people then was to either decide to follow or not to follow. That's what kept me going: having a vision. Plus, I learned early with my dad as my role model how to manage time, and I learned to handle a particular item one time, get rid of it, and then move on to the next item. If I got a letter in the mail, for example, I would read it, respond to it, and then discard it. I didn't have to worry about that stacking up and becoming a part of what hindered me from doing the work that needed to be done.

JAMES: *That's incredible. What was it that brought you to Utah in the first place?*

REV. DAVIS: I was born in Georgia and grew up going to segregated Black schools in high school. Then I went to Tuskegee, which was an all-Black college, and then I was drafted in the Army. I decided the Air Force was a better place. I enlisted and went in for four years. When I got out, I decided that maybe college was important, and I finished. I enrolled in lots of colleges, four or five at a time, taking a full load in California and Northern California, the Oakland area. When I graduated from UC Berkeley, one of those many colleges, there was a professor here in Salt Lake, who read about this crazy UC Berkeley student that was taking seventy hours per semester. He invited me to come to Salt Lake. I came in 1972 to teach communications, and then I taught communications at the university for forty-two years.

JAMES: *So, going back to how you learned to manage time from your dad, that's probably the only way you were able to manage seventy hours of credits per semester.*

REV. DAVIS: The only way you can possibly manage that number of hours of college credit is to be able to manage your time well. You have to be able to manage one thing and be done with it. That's also true about church. You have to learn how to deal with a funeral, and when the funeral is over, go to a wedding, and when the wedding is over, go to a birthday party, and when the birthday party is over, go to choir rehearsal. You have to do one piece at a time.

JAMES: *So, what were you trying to accomplish doing all that school in such a short amount of time?*

REV. DAVIS: One of the things I believe, and that my father drilled into us, is that to make it in this society as an African American, you have to be well prepared. I was trying to get myself as well prepared for the work that I would later do as soon as possible. I had lost a lot of time by dropping out of college and going into the military. I had lost years in terms of time, so I had to catch up with my peers. That's why I was taking a lot of courses at four or five different colleges at a time.

JAMES: *I think there are so many different challenges that African Americans have to go through to be at the same level as our counterparts. At that time, the sixties, what challenges did you experience, being Black and going through UC Berkeley?*

REV. DAVIS: It was a lot of fun. It didn't seem to me to be a major challenge. To go to UC Berkeley, Merritt College, Laney College, and Golden Gate Seminary all at the same time, I learned early how to do the work related to a particular subject and use it in multiple ways. For example, if I was writing a paper about African Americans and the press, I'd write that for one class and then adjust it and rewrite it for another class.

JAMES: *Did you find any barriers because you were Black?*

REV. DAVIS: No major barriers. Those came after I was engaged in the work. When I came to Utah, for example, one of the first things that happened to me was to be denied a place to stay. Not only that, but I was escorted off a particular college campus here because I didn't look the part for the role I needed to do. So most of the barriers that I've run into have come either when I was a small child growing up in Georgia or later on in my days of work.

JAMES: *You were denied a place to stay?*

REV. DAVIS: I was called and invited to come take a job here. The University of Utah sent me a list of places they recommended for workers to live in. I picked one, paid a deposit, had a phone installed. When I got here, the landlord said, "Not here." I'm not sure what that was all about. I suspected it was about skin color, but I'm not so sure.

JAMES: *So was it a job that brought you to Salt Lake? Or what did you do before coming here? Did you know much about Utah?*

REV. DAVIS: I knew nothing about Utah prior to the invitation. Perhaps I'd heard of it in geography class, but I don't even remember that. I didn't do any research to find out about it. All I knew was that there was a person willing to hire me, sight unseen, without filling out an application, and pay me a good deal of money to come here. So I came on a one-year obligation. Years later, I'm still here.

JAMES: *What made you decide to stay?*

REV. DAVIS: I saw there was an overwhelming need here in Utah, that there were more problems here, that this state was behind in terms of Civil Rights and in terms of human rights and the needs of people. It was behind places like California, even places like Georgia, where I grew up. I decided, along with my wife, that we would stay here and do what we could to help bring about positive change for the good of the ten thousand or so African Americans who were living in Utah at the time.

There were ten of us that had to come to Utah at the same time, in 1972. I'm the only one of the ten who's still here. I stayed because somebody needed to do something to help people get an education, find scholarship funds, change the laws, work with the legislature, and work in academic institutions.

JAMES: *What made you decide to take those steps?*

REV. DAVIS: Well, I was well prepared. I had spent time in Berkeley and then Oakland in the military and other places. That's what allowed me to make the commitment to stay here. Plus, Calvary Baptist Church became available at the same time, and I was prepared to be a pastor of the church, already ordained prior to coming here. With the opening at Calvary and at the university, that gave me the impetus for wanting to stay.

JAMES: *What do you feel was one of your biggest accomplishments?*

REV. DAVIS: In the early days, it was working with the legislature to help them understand that Martin Luther King Jr. did, in fact, come to Utah, that there was a need for everybody to be treated equally, regardless of what their skin color might look like. Also, I wanted to ensure that there was fair housing available for persons who wanted to live here in the state of Utah, so I think those were my first major achievements. And those kinds of things have continued, even until now. I've been working with the housing authority for Salt Lake City, I helped to raise the funds to build the housing project on Fifth, which is for homeless veterans, and I helped to institute feeding programs for those who are homeless and hungry. That's all the way up until today. I'm still part of a committee appointed by the mayor, the chairman of the council, and the police chief to deal with racial equity and fairness and policing here in the city of Salt Lake.

JAMES: *How has the murder of George Floyd affected your activity and outreach?*

REV. DAVIS: My schedule blew up. I got called upon to be on boards and committees. I got called on to meet with different groups. I met with all the athletic people at the university, for example, and at BYU, I have worked with several businesses to help them understand how they might change their usual way of doing things to a better way that's more inclusive.

Major impacts have resulted. The mayor has adjusted her budget requests to include more for African Americans' equity in terms of the police department and even her own office. The University of Utah has hired a public safety director and a police chief who was African American. So we've seen major changes occur, but we still have major work to do in the area of corrections. The overwhelming number of people, percentage-wise, in the prisons is still African Americans. Though we have a law that says people ought to be treated more equitably, African Americans tend to be the object of corrections at every level—arrest, court, conviction, and then imprisonment.

JAMES: *I feel like that's something you've been working on a long time.*

REV. DAVIS: I've been working on corrections issues since 1978. I was the first African American appointed by the governor to serve as a member of the board of corrections and the first African American to be chair of the policymaking arm of the Utah Board of Corrections. So I've been working in that area for many years. We were the ones who decided, for example, that there ought to be halfway houses, that we ought to help people safely and successfully reintegrate into society.

JAMES: *To go back to you being pastor for forty-five years of Calvary Baptist Church, the oldest Black Baptist church in the state of Utah, what impact have our Black churches have here?*

REV. DAVIS: Well, for Black Utahns living here, the Black church is the gathering place. It's where you can go and find large numbers of African Americans. There are about thirty African American churches in the state of Utah, and all of them are here on the Wasatch Front, within forty miles of where we are currently seated. Those are the gathering places. They are the organizing places, the places that cast a vision about what issues need to be dealt with. Then they enlist people to deal with them. One of the things I'm working on currently, for example, is the disparities in terms of health care. That's a project where the Calvary Baptist Church has joined with the Native American Indian Walk-In Center, the Hispanic community, the Polynesian community, the African refugee community, and the other health departments to say we need to make sure that people get equitable treatment. That disparity was really highlighted when COVID-19 came along.

JAMES: *I saw that Calvary is where people can go get tests and vaccinations. It's great to see the church not only just as a place of worship but also as a community hub. It's a place where you can get connected to a lot of resources. People will give us a call at the chamber because they're looking for a church or a barber shop.*

REV. DAVIS: Those resources have always been there in addition to religion and faith. Calvary was started to help teach people how to read and write during the late 1800s. We've always emphasized education, health care, political involvement, and social interactions. Those primary purposes go along with the religious purpose of the African American churches, those thirty churches that exist. They are Baptist, Methodist, God in Christ, Seventh Day Adventists. They are apostolic, they are independent congregations, and all of them work together to ensure not only that people are saved, but also that their lives are healthy and have meaning.

JAMES: *What are some examples of how different faiths work together?*

REV. DAVIS: We meet together to talk about issues, and we go up to the Capitol and talk to the politicians about the needs of the community. In addition to that, we have fellowship on a regular basis. Almost every week, other than the first Sunday, there was a fellowship at one of the churches, regardless of whether the denomination was the same or not. You won't find that true in places like California or Chicago—Baptists stay with Baptists or Methodists with Methodists. Even in Las Vegas, where there are a ton of churches on the West Side, people tend to stay with their particular denomination instead of working together. In the year 2002, when the Olympics came here, it was the churches that came together to form a united religious organization to work with the Olympics.

JAMES: *What do you feel makes this place different? I know you've talked before about how the churches work together because there is so much influence by the LDS church—and you've also talked about how cooperative they are, too—but why do you see Utah as a great place to live?*

REV. DAVIS: Well, first of all, the economy is diverse, jobs are available, and you can get employment without much of a problem here. Secondly, there are those who dominate the community and culture, but they bend over backwards to help the least and last in the community. That makes a tremendous difference.

JAMES: *What do you say to those who don't see that help or who feel like they're not being heard?*

REV. DAVIS: I would remind them that, as we work together, we're able to achieve a lot in this community and in the world at large. For example, when Katrina hit, people of different denominations, different religious backgrounds, and different political persuasions were working together in order to help the people who were affected negatively by that storm. I would say to people that you need to open your eyes. Take a look, and you will discover that there's more good going for us here than in many other places. I traveled all over the world, and I have people who say to me constantly, "You guys are doing more about Black history, more to help African Americans, in Utah than we are in Chicago or than we are in Oakland, California."

" As we work together, we're able to achieve a lot in this community and in the world at large. "

—REV. DR. FRANCE DAVIS

PASTOR COREY HODGES

Pastor of The Point Church, a Multicultural Christian community in Salt Lake City, chaplain for the NBA Utah Jazz professional basketball team, and a columnist for The Salt Lake Tribune faith section for five years, Rev. Corey Hodges has been a guiding light to many in the community and in the Christian faith.

JAMES: *So, Pastor Hodges, talk to us about what you see in the community right now.*

PASTOR HODGES: It seems like some young people move here and they are on that track upward, corporately. It seems like it's happening a little quicker than it used to. For young Black families, I'm telling people all the time that this place is the best kept secret in the world. There are so many opportunities. Of course, those opportunities come with expectations. What are you going to do? Are you going to be faithful to this community, sow seeds of loyalty and progress and give of yourself and also give your family some time, right? We know people have moved here, and have done really well—young Black families doing really well. They do seem to be plugging in a little faster.

JAMES: *You've been a pastor for twenty-five years. You're seasoned but still young yourself at the same time.*

PASTOR HODGES: It's been fun and interesting. I would say more opportunities are coming my way. The churches are more established now, so I have time to do other things outside the church. Before, I felt like I needed to really focus and make sure the church was healthy and growing. I had opportunities years back that I turned down because I felt like I needed to focus. So now I feel a little more free to accept some more community appointments, like the gubernatorial appointment. And the Jazz—that's something fun, right? The chaplain that preceded me was there, believe it or not, for thirty years—Jerry Lewis, who was the pastor of Point Christian Church. He passed away, and then they contacted me, and I was happy to do it. It's an opportunity to do something positive for Christ in the lives of these young millionaires, you know, and then I think, as it relates to the chamber, we can see the Jazz is trying to diversify as well, getting more African American players and foreign players too. I think that was also an avenue to create relationships. A Black dude from Oklahoma or Texas or Florida is coming to play for the Jazz and will be connected with an African American pastor. I'm not saying that's what happened, but I am saying that's one of the advantages of having an African American chaplain here to acclimate them to town. I think African Americans have a great deal of respect for a pastor; that's just kind of in our DNA as people. So I've been enjoying doing that and getting other pastors sometimes to come down to help me out there—forty-plus home games so far, not to mention the away games.

JAMES: *I feel like you can wear multiple hats at the same time, being a Black pastor, having been not only the chaplain for the Jazz but also someone who can connect them to the community and businesses. You can help them find out where to get their hair cut, all of that.*

PASTOR HODGES: I think that's on all of us who support the chamber, right? We want to help those new people navigate, find a church, find a barbershop, find soul food places. I enjoy doing it. I think if you've got small kids, I can't think of a better place right now to raise kids than Utah. I do wear multiple hats because I don't feel like I'm just a pastor. I feel obligated to the community that's given me so much to help other young African Americans make it here. That's whether you're coming to the Jazz, Goldman Sachs, or Google. I just saw that huge Amazon plan, too, out on Route 90. So that's going to be a growth area. So as people come in and connect, I feel like I'm not just a pastor but also a citizen of this community. I'm going to use the equity that God has blessed me with to make sure that other young Black families connect.

> " I feel obligated to the community that's given me so much to help other young African Americans make it here. That's whether you're coming to the Jazz, Goldman Sachs, or Google. "
>
> —PASTOR COREY HODGES

JAMES: *The role of a pastor in Utah is a little different than the role of a pastor elsewhere. When you have a small community, I feel like a lot more opportunities and commitments come your way.*

PASTOR HODGES: I think that's not just true in a religious community; it's true everywhere. It's not a crowded field, so you get opportunities here that you may not get in other places. I don't think that should be an excuse for us to be mediocre or substandard. I think that is a reason for us to really make sure we're sharp and we're prepared because you will get opportunities here in the capital city; right? I looked at it when I came as a young man as, *Hey, you've really got to sharpen your tools because you could* *find yourself in the governor's mansion in some way. The more you define yourself, the more you have an opportunity to represent yourself and your families well so people will listen to what we have to say.*

I do think the role of pastor is a little different, and that's why I wanted to let you know France Davis's legacy here is so important because Black people needed an advocate. I don't think anyone did better than he did, even if you look across the country and look at African American pastors who held a torch for equality and equity and just made sure that we were treated fairly. We have fifty years of carrying that torch, and he carried it well. When I came here, it was easy to stand on somebody's shoulders like that. I tried to compliment the work he has done.

I've been thinking about activism as you obviously know, with national events like George Floyd. I think in Utah, you feel so small, with the African American population around 1 percent. I think I paid a little more attention to it than I probably would have if I were in another state with higher diversity. As a pastor, the social part and social activism and responsibility is there, and I've certainly got to use my influence as a pastor to help in that area. I think all pastors in this area, in terms of Brown and Black pastors, we have to stay motivated. So, yes, the role of pastor, in my mind, is a little more expansive here in a lot of ways.

JAMES: *Talk to us a little bit about how churches are changing, how worship is changing. The landscape for how people serve the Lord has changed so much. Do you feel that the traditional Southern Baptist way is always going to stay the same?*

PASTOR HODGES: I think you said earlier it's not good or bad or right or wrong—it's just different. It's the *not a monolith* idea. I think, across the board, number one, we see the ethnic lines culturally are getting blurred, right? So you have white kids listening to hip-hop. You've got little Black girls playing tennis and golf. Even gospel music, for instance, is very diverse. You've got Maverick City, Travis Greene, Jonathan Nelson—white people and Black people listen to this music. I think church life is kind of the same. I don't think we are ever going to—nor should we ever—lose our traditional rules. We've got to keep, you know, *Amazing Grace.* We've got to keep the ushers and the choir. There's great value and history in that. At the same time, I think we've got to have other options. I think we have to embrace the diversity within our own ethnic group.

People criticize the traditional way. People criticize the contemporary way. It's just a matter of choice, a matter of preference. I think we will never lose the traditional roots of African Americanism as it relates to church. At the same time, we all should be better, make sure that our people have quality choices available. There are some things about Blackness and Black people that won't change. The question is: What are the things that need to be preserved? Even if you're progressive or contemporary, I think there are values—respecting our elders, singing some hymns—we need to protect. Once we have those discussions and debates—and they might be vigorous—I think the future of the Black church looks promising. Jesus Christ is at the center of all those things. That message, I think, can never go away, but there is room to grow.

A leader in the corporate sphere as the former president and CEO of Maxam North America, Stanton Johnson and his family also found deep ties to church families in Utah when they immigrated here from Liberia. He's been a longtime deacon at Calvary Baptist Church and was a deacon at New Pilgrim Baptist Church before that. Here, he shares some of his family's experience in finding a home church.

JAMES: *So I know you're entrenched in Calvary Baptist Church, but you didn't start there, right?*

STANTON: One thing that we were really particular about when we first came to Utah is finding where our kids are going to go to church. In a state that is less than 1 percent Black, the schools are going to be predominantly white. I was looking for a church that would provide the same kind of experience I had growing up, a small Black Baptist church that would give them a whole different perspective about their faith. We found New Pilgrim Baptist Church. We were there for ten to twelve years.

JAMES: *Talk about the spiritual experience as well as your growth there. Obviously, your spiritual background is very important to you.*

STANTON: Without that spiritual background, you have really no basis for how to live, and we are people of faith. In Liberia, I was born into the Presbyterian Church. My father was an elder; my mother was an elder. We believe that certain things happen because of our faith in God. So we truly believe, especially with a dominant faith here in Utah, that our kids should know what it means to believe the way we do.

JAMES: *Do you feel like being a Black Baptist here would have been different than attending a Black Baptist church anywhere in the country or even in Liberia?*

STANTON: Well, in Liberia, I was actually Presbyterian. I know there are many Presbyterian churches here in Utah, and we were trying to see if we could identify with any of them. I didn't really find it—the same hymns and things like that.

JAMES: *So you raised three kids here and have had a successful career in the mining industry. You found a church community that has been there for you. I love your whole story, starting out as an immigrant and thriving here.*

STANTON: It's been God's favor. Work ethic is important, and then, of course, my service in the church. I do not value regular hours. As a deacon at Pilgrim, I was responsible for all of their financials and then as a deacon at Calvary. I've had the favor, and we just want to keep it going. The problem sometimes is finding young people who are willing to go into the church and be active or become a deacon. We need to continue to encourage our youth and help them understand that they can do anything. We have to help them understand they have so many options, professionally and in society and in our churches.

> " We need to continue to encourage our youth and help them understand that they can do anything. "

—STANTON JOHNSON

Conclusion

Utah's diversity may be small, but so is the overall community. The entire population of Utah is less than some of the more popular cities in the country. The state seems big on the map, but it's mostly filled with national parks, mountains, and water. Most of the population lies alongside the Great Salt Lake where Green Flake told Brigham Young, "This is the Place." When you arrive and become connected, you'll find "Small Lake City," two degrees of separation of connections, welcoming and willing to share and create opportunities. You get almost the best of both worlds—small community and city feel.

The Black community may be the smallest in Utah, but we have so many incredible Black leaders, our influence is much larger. The individuals who contributed in this book are just a small sampling of the many contributors to Utah's thriving Black community. Since the chamber's inception in 2009 to present, we have seen a rapidly changing and growing Black community who are seeing the possibilities and potential of what Utah can provide. From small business to tech, restaurants, and entertainment, opportunities are growing every day. People didn't like the lack of diversity in Utah and wouldn't stick around. Now, we are seeing people who see the opportunity and are becoming pioneers for change.

Less and less is Utah being viewed as a "hidden gem" and slowly being recognized as the best place for many things—business, opportunity, the outdoors, lifestyle—and one of the most welcoming. When people thought of Black people in Utah, the Utah Jazz was the first to come to mind for most. They represented the Black population for several years. Some still think they do today, but the population is so much more vast and diverse and becoming significant contributors to Utah's overall growth and influence. There is still so much work to be done, and while it may seem challenging to navigate or even find the diverse community in Utah in the beginning, you'll find a collaborative, creative, and thriving community ready and able to change the world. This is Black Utah.

Utah Black Chamber board with Executive Director
James Jackson after receiving the Salt Lake Chamber's
prestigious President's Excellence Award

In 2020, three members of the Utah Black Chamber's leadership were recognized by Utah Business Magazine's Forty under 40

Acnkowledgments

From concept to publishing, this book was developed in less than a year. Strategizing, interviews, promotions, sponsorships, design, formatting, and writing this book in the timeline committed was no easy feat, and a very special thanks to everyone who made this happen.

First, and foremost to my family, especially my fiancée, Michelle, who has supported me from the very beginning and has been a part of my personal growth. The Utah Black Chamber board of directors has a culture unmatched by any other board I have engaged with and who has pushed the chamber's influence and platform to where it is today. Special thank you to their support, vision, and commitment.

To all the contributors who took time out of their busy schedule to meet with me in person, during a challenging time for an hour interview, thank you for sharing your story. The Utah Black Chamber and community appreciates your leadership and commitment to elevating Black Utah.

Thank you to the Young OG perspective, Lonzo Oliver, for recording the interviews and all the sponsors that helped make this happen—Intermountain Healthcare, Workers Compensation Fund, and Zions Bank—and all distribution outlets. The vision of this book grew bigger as the support came flowing in.

We hope this book not only elevates Black Utah but also shines a light on Utah's growing diversity and the strength of its community.

About the Publisher

Soul Excellence Publishing is an independent hybrid publisher founded by Kayleigh O'Keefe. The publisher helps CEOs, founders, executives, and entrepreneurs turn their wisdom into culture-shaping books. Some of the company's international best-selling titles include: *Leading Through the Pandemic: Unconventional Wisdom from Heartfelt Leaders*, *Significant Women: Leaders Reveal What Matters Most*, *The X-Factor: Spiritual Secrets Behind Successful Executives & Entrepreneurs*.

A special thank you to the entire team who made the vision for this book a reality: Kecia Bal, ghostwriting; Rosemi Mederos, copyediting; Lewelin Polanco, interior design; and Natalie Gleason, marketing.

Website: https://soulexcellencepublishing.com/

Made in the USA
Coppell, TX
28 January 2022

72203568R00151